CAMBRIDGE MUSIC HANDBOOKS

Haydn: *The Creation*

CAMBRIDGE MUSIC HANDBOOKS

GENERAL EDITOR: Julian Rushton

Cambridge Music Handbooks provide accessible introductions to major musical works, written by the most informed commentators in the field.

With the concert-goer, performer and student in mind, the books present essential information on the historical and musical context, the composition, and the performance and reception history of each work, or group of works, as well as critical discussion of the music.

Other published titles

Bach: Mass in B Minor JOHN BUTT
Berg: Violin Concerto ANTHONY POPLE
Handel: *Messiah* DONALD BURROWS

Haydn: *The Creation*

Nicholas Temperley
Professor of Music
University of Illinois

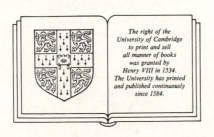

The right of the
University of Cambridge
to print and sell
all manner of books
was granted by
Henry VIII in 1534.
The University has printed
and published continuously
since 1584.

Cambridge University Press
Cambridge
New York   Port Chester
Melbourne   Sydney

Published by the Press Syndicate of the University of Cambridge
The Pitt Building, Trumpington Street, Cambridge CB2 1RP
40 West 20th Street, New York, NY 10011, USA
10 Stamford Road, Oakleigh, Melbourne 3166, Australia

© Cambridge University Press 1991

First published 1991

Printed in Great Britain at the University Press, Cambridge

British Library cataloguing in publication data

Temperley, Nicholas, *1932–*
Haydn: The Creation. – (Cambridge music handbooks)
1. Austrian music. Haydn, Joseph, 1732–1809
I. Title
782.23092

Library of Congress cataloguing in publication data

Temperley, Nicholas.
Haydn, The Creation / Nicholas Temperley.
p.   cm. – (Cambridge music handbooks)
Includes bibliographical references and index.
ISBN 0 521 37255 0 – ISBN 0 521 37865 6 (pbk)
1. Haydn, Joseph, 1732–1809. Schöpfung. I. Title. II. Series.
ML410.H4T36 1991
782.23–dc20   90–1859   CIP MN

ISBN 0–521–372550 hardback
ISBN 0–521–378656 paperback

Contents

Preface   *page* vii

1 *Background*   1
    The Viennese oratorio   1
    The English oratorio   3
    Haydn's career   4
    Haydn's oratorios   5

2 *Theology*   9
    Religion in Georgian England   10
    Religion in Catholic Austria   15
    Haydn's religion   16

3 *The libretto*   19
    Authorship   19
    Sources, structure and revision   20
    Literary character   24
    Translation and adaptation   26

4 *Composition, performance and reception*   31
    Genesis and composition   31
    First performances in Vienna   35
    Publication   36
    First London performances   39
    Early Paris performances   40
    First American performances   41
    Critical reception   42

5 *Design of the work*   47
    Overall plan   47
    Musical unity   49
    Text and musical treatment   52

v

6 *Musical analysis* 65
    Secco recitative 65
    Accompanied recitative 66
    Arias and ensembles 69
    Choruses 78
    Orchestral movements 82
    The Hymn 84

7 *Excerpts from critical essays* 89
    Carl Friedrich Zelter (1802) 89
    William Gardiner (1811) 93
    Thomas Busby (1819) 94
    Edward Taylor[?] (1834) 95
    P.L.A. (1846) 96
    George Alexander Macfarren (1854) 96
    Hugo Wolf (1885) 98
    Paul Dukas (1904) 100
    Heinrich Schenker (1926) 100
    Donald Francis Tovey (1934) 103
    Karl Geiringer (1963) 106
    Charles Rosen (1972) 107

Appendix 1: *Performance practice* 109
    Venue 109
    Language 109
    Vocal soloists 110
    Choral forces 110
    Orchestral forces 111
    Continuo realization 113
    Tempo 114
    Embellishment 115
    Standard ornaments .115
    Dynamics and articulation 116

Appendix 2: *Editions currently available and numbering of
    movements* 118

Notes 121

Bibliography 129

Index 132

Preface

In 1950 I had my first lessons in music history, from Dr Sydney Watson. He chose *The Creation* as one of the great landmarks of European music. He spoke of it warmly but defensively. But for me it needed no defence, as I had immediately fallen in love with it.

After an intervening period, when I thought I was learning to look at music more dispassionately, Edward Olleson's article of 1968 aroused my interest in the English text, that butt of so many green-room and vestry chuckles. I was led to write an article on the subject, and then to publish a new edition, where I tried to deal with the text problem from first principles. Such a background could well explain this book's distinctly English slant, which will not escape the reader's notice. But I maintain that the English aspect is exactly the one that has been unduly neglected in the long history of *Creation* criticism and scholarship. At the same time I have tried to make this a balanced survey; I hope that no significant aspect of the oratorio has been slighted.

I owe a considerable debt to Edward Olleson, for reasons already given; to Susan Homewood of Peters Edition (London), for drawing attention to some interesting anomalies in the course of revising my edition; to Valerie Goertzen, for assisting me in my research; to A. Peter Brown, for telling me about some of his discoveries before they appeared in print; to David Gilbert, for examining the Choudens vocal score in Paris; and to Stephen Whiting, for help with translations. I am also indebted to the staff of many libraries – more particularly that of the British Library, for supplying microfilms of sources and for permission to reproduce the title page of the first edition. Finally, I acknowledge with deep gratitude the repeated assistance of the Research Board of the University of Illinois.

Background

Haydn completed his greatest work, *Die Schöpfung/The Creation*, in 1797, when he was sixty-five years old. It is generally seen as the culmination of his career, although his earlier achievements were centred not in oratorio but in music for orchestra, strings and keyboard, and to a lesser extent in operas, masses and secular songs.

The immediate occasion for the work was a commissioned private performance in Vienna, to be followed by public performances in the same city. Yet *The Creation* bears little affinity to the Italian or German oratorios that had been current in Vienna in Haydn's lifetime, nor does it have any close precedent in his earlier works. Its true ancestor is the English oratorio of Handel, a form which Haydn absorbed and remoulded in the light of his long and unequalled experience as a composer of symphonies and operas.

Oratorio, in the eighteenth century, was closer to the theatre than to the church. The libretto was usually in verse, and was taken from a biblical or other religious story. It provided for arias, recitatives, choruses and an opening sinfonia of the same general character as those found in Italian *opera seria*, and the vocal and instrumental forces were also similar, although there were usually more choruses than in an opera. Oratorios were more at home in theatres or concert halls than in churches – typically, in Lent or Advent, when operas and plays were considered unsuitable; but they were generally performed without action or costumes.

The Viennese oratorio

Vienna was the political, economic and cultural centre of a large, preponderantly Roman Catholic region, monarchically ruled, in which German was the dominant though not the only vernacular language. However, from early in the seventeenth century Vienna's high musical culture had been dominated by Italian influence, which was only beginning to wane in the last two decades of the eighteenth century. Italian-language oratorios were regularly performed in the Emperor's chapel until about 1740, and thereafter in the palaces of the Viennese aristocracy.

With the establishment in 1771 of the Tonkünstler-Societät, a charity for the widows and orphans of musicians, Italian oratorios were also performed in public theatres during the Lent and Advent concert seasons.[1] Haydn himself contributed one of the most successful of these, *Il ritorno di Tobia* (1775), which will be discussed below; another was Mozart's *Il Davidde penitente* (1785). Italian operas were typically two-part dramatic works, based on librettos by Pietro Metastasio (1698–1782) and his imitators which formed a well-knit heroic drama out of a religious story, generally from the Old Testament. The music was largely made up of da capo arias and recitatives, with very few ensembles or choruses.[2]

Around 1780, however, there was a change of taste in the direction of German oratorio in Austria (just as there was, for a time, in opera: Mozart's *Die Entführung aus dem Serail* was composed for the new German Opera House in 1782). From 1779 onwards the Tonkünstler-Societät began to perform works in German. Some of these, such as Johann Georg Albrechtsberger's *Die Pilgrime auf Golgatha* (1781) and Johann Leopold Eybler's *Die Hirten bei der Krippe zu Bethlehem* (1794), owe much to the sentimental, Pietistic type cultivated in Protestant north Germany, a genre that Howard Smither has called the 'lyric oratorio'.[3] Indeed, Haydn's *Die sieben letzten Worte unseres Erlösers am Kreuze* (*The Seven Last Words*), though in many respects a unique phenomenon, belongs if anywhere in this tradition.

One of the first works to be heard in German at the Society's concerts was a translation of Handel's English oratorio *Judas Maccabaeus*,[4] in 1779. A seminal influence in this new development was the Baron Gottfried van Swieten (1733–1803), who may have been responsible for the translation. As Austrian ambassador to the court at Berlin from 1770 to 1777 he had heard choral masterpieces of both Handel and Bach at the concerts given by Princess Anna Amalia. On his return he began to sponsor performances of both composers' works at the Imperial Library, and in about 1785 he organized a society of aristocratic patrons, the Gesellschaft der Associierten, which sponsored private performances of oratorios, mainly Handel's. For this purpose he commissioned Mozart to arrange four of the most popular Handel oratorios with modernized orchestration (1788–90). Later the society commissioned Haydn's three German oratorios: *The Seven Last Words* (1796), *The Creation* (1798) and *The Seasons* (1801). From the Austrian point of view, *The Creation* was a part of the movement for the assertion of German language and culture, first in opposition to the alien Italian opera and oratorio, and later also in defiance of the Napoleonic military threat.

The English oratorio

By contrast with Vienna, London was the mercantile capital of a growing empire ruled by a constitutional monarchy, where a moderate Protestantism prevailed, but did not prevent a dynamic interchange of ideas: freedom of speech, writing and religion were well established, though not absolute. Oratorio in English was essentially the invention of George Frideric Handel (1685–1759). Drawing on a long experience in England from 1710 onwards, he forged a new synthesis from Italian opera and oratorio and English ceremonial and cathedral music. He himself had already mastered all these forms and styles before he entered on his main development of the English oratorio in 1733. The product he created found a permanent welcome with the English public.

The typical Handel oratorio, represented by such masterpieces as *Athalia* (1733), *Saul* (1738), *Samson* (1742), *Belshazzar* (1744), *Judas Maccabaeus* (1746), *Solomon* (1748) and *Jephtha* (1751), is a setting of a dramatic poem in three parts, based on a familiar Old Testament story. The music is made up of recitatives, airs, ensembles and choruses, with much freedom of form; the chorus plays a prominent part as protagonist or moralizer or both. A few Handel oratorios are on secular subjects. Two sacred oratorios that ultimately became the most famous of all, *Israel in Egypt* (1738) and *Messiah* (1742), depart from the standard pattern in using prose librettos compiled directly from the Bible, and in having no implied dramatic action or personified characters. In these two works the chorus plays an even more prominent, indeed the leading, part, and they have a generality, a breadth of human appeal, that brings them closer to *The Creation* than any other of Handel's works.

Winton Dean, the foremost authority on Handel's oratorios, has emphasized the dramatic aspect at the expense of the religious, and has presented a strong case for reviving on the stage the ones that were dramatically conceived (a practice that was not permitted in Handel's time).[5] The cuts he recommends, and his choices among different versions, are designed to enhance dramatic and human interest; and he interprets and judges the oratorios almost wholly in terms of the theatre.

Dean's advocacy has succeeded splendidly in stimulating fresh appreciation of Handel in a modern world more attuned to drama than to religion. As a historical theory, however, it has distorted the evidence by systematically playing down the moral and religious significance of the oratorios. In particular, *Israel in Egypt* and *Messiah* (excluded altogether from Dean's study because they were not 'dramatic') are profound expressions of orthodox Anglican religion in a time of controversy. This side of the matter has been illuminated by the work of Ruth Smith; it will be discussed in chapter 2.

The success of Handel's oratorios with the English public was unparalleled, and spread to all parts of the country, all classes of society, and eventually almost all religious denominations. He came to be regarded as Britain's national composer. In the later eighteenth century, performances of Handel's oratorios took on more and more ritual grandeur; they began to move from the theatre to the church, and to employ larger and larger forces. The trend had been started by Handel himself, who instituted performances of *Messiah* in the Foundling Hospital chapel, and who, according to William Hayes, performed oratorios 'with at least double the Number of Voices and Instruments than ever were heard in a Theatre before'.[6] It reached a culminating point with the great Handel Commemoration festivals in Westminster Abbey from 1784 to 1791, at which the total number of performers gradually increased from 525 to 1068.[7]

In addition, Handel's oratorios continued to be performed regularly in the London theatres during Lent, and at provincial choral festivals, with more modest numbers; extracts were performed as anthems and as songs, and were arranged as hymn tunes and organ pieces; and they became to the English, as no music has before or since, the focus of patriotic and religious feeling, and the standard by which all other serious music was judged. No English oratorio had the slightest chance of challenging Handel's, and even a composer as famous and popular as Haydn was thought presumptuous to set his work up as a rival to his great predecessor's.

Haydn's career

Franz Joseph Haydn was born at Rohrau, Austria, in 1732, and he spent most of his life in the neighbourhood of Vienna. Educated in the choir school attached to St Stephen's cathedral, he worked for a number of years as a freelance performer. In 1761 he received the chief appointment of his career, as kapellmeister to the Esterházy family. For the next three decades he lived almost wholly in the palaces of these extremely wealthy princes, first at Eisenstadt, and then, after 1767, at the still grander palace newly built at Esterháza – which, although in Hungary, was still quite close to Vienna and within the Habsburg domains. He was permitted only an occasional visit to Vienna; but, as he said himself, it was his isolation that forced him to be original. By the time his freedom came in 1790 (due to the accession of a prince who placed little value on Haydn's musical activity), he had become the most famous composer in Europe, and had established the norms of classical music in the symphony, the string quartet and the keyboard sonata.

Haydn experienced the overwhelming emotional effect of Handel's oratorios during his London visits of 1791–2 and 1793–4, and saw for himself how they appealed not merely to a group of *cognoscenti* like Swieten's circle in Vienna, but to a large mass of mainly middle-class people who responded as one body to the ineffable sublimity of the music. His first experience of this novel sensation was at the 1791 Handel Festival at Westminster Abbey:[8] the programme included two performances of *Israel in Egypt*, which of all Handel's oratorios depends most on monumental choruses and vivid word-painting, plus *Messiah* and excerpts from several others.

There are many accounts of Haydn's reaction to this event. According to one of his early biographers, he 'confessed . . . that when he heard the music of Hendl [*sic*] in London, he was struck as if he had been put back to the beginning of his studies and had known nothing up to that moment. He meditated on every note and drew from those most learned scores the essence of true muscial grandeur.'[9] As an eminent Haydn scholar has put it, 'He found a whole nation aroused by compositions offered in monumental performances . . . . He desired intensely to write, as Handel had written, works meant for a whole nation.'[10] The results of this seminal experience are to be found in *The Creation*: in the simplicity of its musical diction, in its imaginative tone-painting, above all in its great choruses of praise.

After his final return to Austria in 1794, Haydn enjoyed almost another decade of full composing activity, of which *The Creation* was the crowning monument. He lived in Vienna until his death in 1809.

Haydn's oratorios

Oratorio was no part of Haydn's duties at the Esterházy court, and his first effort in the genre was the Italian oratorio commissioned by the Vienna Tonkünstler-Societät for performance in 1775, *Il ritorno di Tobia*. Howard

Smither, who has made a thorough study of this work, regards it as 'an outstanding example of the late-eighteenth-century Italian oratorio',[11] though it might be argued that the competition is less than formidable. *Tobia* had a new libretto, along Metastasian lines, by Giovanni Gastone Boccherini (1742–*c*. 1800), brother of the composer Luigi Boccherini.

The story is adapted from the Book of Tobit (part of the Catholic, though not of the Protestant, Bible). The chief element of dramatic tension is caused by the hope that the blind Tobit, father of Tobias, will have his sight restored; it is resolved by the miraculous intervention of the angel Raphael, who has been participating in the action in disguise. Apart from the subject matter, the absence of amorous entanglements, and the two-act structure, this libretto differs little from that of a contemporary *opera seria*, and Haydn set it in much the same way as he would have set an opera text. There are only three choruses (two more were added for a 1784 revival), no ensembles except for one duet, long recitatives (both *secco* and *accompagnato*), and many coloratura passages. The chief marks of Haydn's individuality are the surprisingly rich orchestration (taking full advantage of the Society's resources) and the inventive tone-painting, several examples of which are cited by Smither.[12]

Tobia was a notable success, so much so that it has been suggested that it resulted in Haydn's being kept out of the Society for many years by jealous rivals. One of many favourable press comments seems significant: 'Especially his choruses glowed with a fire that was otherwise only in Handel.'[13] It is not known to what extent Haydn at this early date was familiar with Handel's music but, as Smither points out, both the tone-painting and the learned fugues associated with the older master are present in the *Tobia* choruses of 1775. They are the only elements in the work that are remotely prophetic of *The Creation*.

Haydn's next oratorio, *The Seven Last Words*, is extraordinary both in its history and in its ultimate form. In about 1785 Haydn was commissioned to provide orchestral music for a liturgy of the Passion that was customary at the underground church of Santa Cueva in Cadiz, Spain, in which each of the seven Words spoken by Christ on the cross was the subject of a short sermon by the bishop.[14] In response to this – and with little guidance as to what was really wanted – Haydn composed a work for which there was no historical precedent: a series of seven instrumental one-movement 'sonatas' in different keys, all in slow tempo, each beginning with a theme inspired by a Latin text (which was underlaid); the whole preceded by a slow introduction and concluding with a *Terremoto* (earthquake).

The work was privately performed in 1787 in Vienna and other cities, and in the same year was published in versions for orchestra, for keyboard, and for string quartet. All three became immensely popular; it is in the string quartet version, made by the composer himself, that it has been best known. Haydn probably would have been content to leave it at that. But in 1795, soon after his return from London, he heard in Passau Cathedral a choral arrangement of *The Seven Last Words* that had been made without his knowledge by the local kapellmeister, Joseph Friebert (1723–99), who was a composer of some experience.

Friebert had used a German text of the pietistic type, partly based on Carl Wilhelm Ramler's well known oratorio *Tod Jesu* (set most notably by Carl Heinrich Graun at Berlin in 1755). Friebert simply superimposed a four-part chorus on Haydn's orchestral score, repeating certain portions as ritornellos, and later added accompanied recitatives between the sonatas.

Haydn was quite impressed by Friebert's version. He took a copy home to Vienna and then made his own rearrangement of the choral version in 1795–6. Essentially, he accepted most of Friebert's added vocal parts but rejected the added ritornellos and accompanied recitatives completely. Later he added wind parts and, with the help of Swieten, made many alterations in Friebert's text. Instead of the accompanied recitatives he wrote an unmetred *a capella* choral setting of each Word, in German translation, as a prelude to the corresponding sonata; but before Sonata 5 he inserted, instead, a newly composed *largo cantabile* for twelve–part winds. In this form, presumably, Haydn's choral version of *The Seven Last Words* was first performed by Swieten's Gesellschaft der Associierten on 26 March 1796. A public performance was presented by the Tonkünstler-Societät on 1 April 1798. It was published, with a bilingual text (German/Italian), in November 1801.

The task of writing music lasting nearly an hour without any real contrast of mood, tempo or texture (save for the concluding *Terremoto*) is one that few composers would have cared to tackle. Haydn's music is heartfelt and moving in the purely instrumental versions, but the choral arrangement, with a text of little poetic merit, tends to dilute the intensity of the original music while failing to supply added variety or interest. However, it is significant that Haydn was occupied with sacred choral music more than anything else in the months immediately preceding the composition of *The Creation*. As well as *The Seven Last Words*, Haydn in 1796 had written two of his great masses, the *Missa Sancti Bernardi de Offida* ('Heiligmesse') and the *Missa in tempore belli* ('Paukenmesse').

In summary, there was not a great deal in Haydn's previous career as a composer to provide real precedent for such a towering masterpiece as *The Creation*. Insofar as any explanation can be attempted, it seems that his experience of Handel's oratorios in London was the chief stimulus and inspiration to this supreme effort of his last years.

Haydn composed one more oratorio, for which Swieten wrote an entirely new libretto, cleverly fashioned from the long and immensely popular English poem *The Seasons* by James Thomson (1700–48). The oratorio was first performed at Vienna in April 1801, and published in May 1802 by Breitkopf and Härtel at Leipzig, together with incredibly bad English and French translations (provided by Swieten) which discouraged the reception of the work in London and Paris.[15] The work is considerably longer than *The Creation*. It is divided into four parts representing the four seasons, and it continues in the general vein of enlightened humanism and naturalism that marked its great predecessor. Some have maintained that it is musically on a more consistently high level than *The Creation*;[16] but, the characters being idealized peasants and the subject matter their lives and experiences, Haydn adjusted his style downwards on the scale that extends from the sublime to the popular, with a consequent gain in intimacy and charm at the expense of greatness.

In *The Creation* we see the greatest composer of the time, at the very height of his powers, gathering all his resources to tackle the central mystery of our existence. It was a supreme moment in musical history. An eminent German musicologist has said of *The Creation* and *The Seasons*: 'With the unique exception of *The Magic Flute*, there are simply no other works of the time in which the universal language spoke in such degree to all mankind or was in such degree understood by all as in these two late oratorios of Haydn.'[17]

2

Theology

In this age we are inclined to treat sacred and secular music on the same footing: as entertainments for our leisure hours, whether in theatre, concert hall or living room. But for a believer, sacred music must always be more than an entertainment, for it deals in matters of life and death. A serious opera may overwhelm the audience's feelings and, for a few hours, give them the illusion that they are participating in heroism or tragedy of the highest order; but it is all over when they wake up the next morning. For non-believers an oratorio has a similar effect, but religious persons may find that it bears on important moral decisions in their own lives, of their relations with their God, and on their hopes for salvation.

In studying religious works, therefore, one should always consider the theological context. Many are written for a specific use as a part of public worship; others can be thought of as personal expressions of the composer's religious feeling. As a rule, an oratorio fits neither of these categories; it constitutes instead a public expression of the religious feeling of a society, whether in narrative, dramatic or contemplative form.

Although Haydn's contribution to *The Creation* obviously far outweighs that of the unidentified librettist in *artistic* importance, it is the libretto that chiefly determines its *theological* character. Music, even the greatest, cannot independently express complex ideas, though it may colour, modify and greatly intensify them. Since, therefore, we are told that the text was originally written for Handel (see chapter 3), it is to early Georgian England that we must look for the primary theological context of the work.

At the same time we must bear in mind that *The Creation* was first performed in Vienna. Swieten presumably decided that the text was suitable for Viennese audiences, though he modified it to an unknown degree; Haydn set it to music and performed it. By these acts Swieten and Haydn offered a religious (as well as an artistic) statement to an accepting public; thus a secondary theological context of the work is to be sought in turn-of-the-century Vienna.

Religion in Georgian England

The time of Handel's major English oratorios (1733–51) was one of relative tranquillity in the English church and state. Religious wars and persecutions were a thing of the past, but it was not, as is often stated, an irreligious age. Rationalism and the discoveries of science were not thought to contradict the teachings of Christianity; indeed, John Locke and Isaac Newton had both argued that science reaffirmed revealed religion. They had approved William Whiston's *New Theory of the Earth* (1696), which had shown that the creation of the world in six days, as described in the Bible, was fully consonant with reason and philosophy. 'To the vast majority ... Newtonianism indicated, exultantly, the proof of a Grand Designer and Regulator of the orderly universe disclosed by Sir Isaac's experiments.'[1] This point of view is nowhere better expressed than in Joseph Addison's free paraphrase of Psalm xix:1–6, first printed in *The Spectator* for 23 August 1712:

> The Spacious Firmament on high,
> With all the blue Etherial Sky,
> And spangled Heav'ns, a Shining Frame,
> Their great Original proclaim:
> Th' unwearied Sun, from day to day,
> Does his Creator's Pow'r display,
> And publishes to every Land
> The Work of an Almighty Hand.
>
> Soon as the Evening Shades prevail,
> The Moon takes up the wondrous Tale,
> And nightly to the listning Earth
> Repeats the Story of her Birth:
> Whilst all the Stars that round her burn,
> And all the Planets, in their turn,
> Confirm the Tidings as they rowl,
> And spread the Truth from Pole to Pole.
>
> What though, in solemn Silence, all
> Move round the dark terrestrial Ball?
> What tho' nor real Voice nor Sound
> Amid their radiant Orbs be found?
> In Reason's Ear they all rejoice,
> And utter forth a glorious Voice,
> For ever singing, as they shine,
> 'The hand that made us is Divine'.

It is surely no coincidence that the same passage from Psalm 19 was the basis for Nos. 12 and 13 of *The Creation*,[2] or that Haydn's famous setting of No. 13, 'The heavens are telling the glory of God', was later made into a hymn tune that was then widely sung to Addison's paraphrase quoted above.[3]

There were those, however – the Deists – who probed further, and asked what scientific proof or rational argument could be found in support of the holy scriptures. In particular, they doubted that the God who had designed this wonderfully orderly universe would have revealed himself to a small obscure tribe such as the Jews. They denied that evidence or reason could support belief in the many miracles and divine interventions in human affairs recounted in the Bible.

The Deists put forward their ideas in a large number of printed books and pamphlets, which were then rebutted in still greater quantity by orthodox Christians, chiefly Anglican. The height of Deist success was in the years 1725–33; the orthodox side began to gain the upper hand in the controversy after 1733. This was just at the time of Handel's oratorios, and Ruth Smith has shown most convincingly that they, and more especially *Messiah*, were strongly motivated by the orthodox response to Deism: they showed 'that God could aid man with miracles; that He had thus aided the Israelites ... and that Jesus fulfilled the Old Testament prophecies of the Messiah'.[4]

The Deists, however, did believe in a divine creator, even if some of them doubted the details of creation given in Genesis. One of their leading spokesmen, Thomas Chubb, stated this clearly: 'That there is a Deity, or governing mind, who gave being to all things external to himself, and who exists by, or from, an absolute necessity, is, to me, most evident and plain. ... I think atheism, in point of argument, is insupportable'.[5] Even the free-thinker David Hume, who attacked both Christians and Deists, asserted in 1757 that 'the whole frame of Nature bespeaks an intelligent author'.[6] Up to that time science had offered no substantial challenge to the biblical account. The Copernican discovery that the earth was only one of a number of planets circling the sun was not thought to contradict Genesis i.16–18: 'And God made two great lights ... And God set them in the firmament of the heaven to give light upon the earth, and to rule over the day and over the night, and to divide the light from the darkness'. It was not until well after mid-century that geology began to challenge the current theory that fossils had been created by Noah's flood, while in biology it was assumed throughout the century that species were immutable. As a leading historian of the period has put it, 'we had best remember that to conceive of a world without a creator, without a plan, and without a purpose, was an incredible thing, until nineteenth-century science made it more plausible ... Order and reason implied an intelligent, purposeful creation.'[7]

On the face of it, then, it would seem that the subject matter of *The Creation* was not a particularly controversial one in the Deist/Anglican dispute. There is one significant passage, however, that asserts God's power and intention to intervene arbitrarily in earthly affairs: this is No. 27, a paraphrase of Psalm civ.27–30. We must conclude that the author was on the 'Anglican' side, then, like most of Handel's librettists. On the other hand, this question is obviously not the main emphasis of the *Creation* text. On the contrary, the broader message seems distinctly 'ecumenical' in its appeal, designed to satisfy both Anglicans and Deists. Moreover it was particularly in harmony with the times in its optimistic emphasis on the wonders of creation, and on man as the lord of the earth, with only brief allusions to the coming Fall (in Nos. 27 and 33). The older sense of the overwhelming burden of sin, expressed in Augustinian and Calvinist theology, had almost entirely disappeared from the Anglican scene: Anglicans were mostly Arminians (believing that every individual could be saved if he sincerely cast himself on Christ's mercy),[8] and John Wesley, whose great revival movement was beginning just at this time, took the same position. It is true that some Dissenting bodies, notably the Independents (Congregationalists), Presbyterians and Particular Baptists, held to their Calvinistic heritage, but this hardly mattered, since they altogether disapproved of oratorio, whether performed in a theatre or in church.

The Creation presents a comfortably optimistic picture of the world and of humanity's place in it. As in the Handel oratorios, 'the terrifying and mysterious Jehovah is replaced by a humanitarian, paternally available God,'[9] surrounded by adoring angels. Haydn shows man and woman in eternally lovely surroundings, and in idyllic innocence, as in a pastoral; and even if Christians in the audience know that the Fall of Man with all its miserable consequences is just round the corner, at least it is banished from the closed world of the oratorio itself.

Of the two versions of the creation story that the Bible provides (Genesis i.1–ii.3 and ii.4–iii.24), the librettist relied almost entirely on the first, with its six days of labour in the making of the natural world, culminating in the creation of man and woman in the image of God. He passed over the second account, the story of the garden of Eden, where Adam and Eve disobey God's command and so set mankind on the path of sin, initiating the need for atonement which is the root of Christian theology. Neither account, of course, could be contested by an orthodox Christian, but the first was far more widely acceptable than the second in the climate of early Georgian England. It celebrates nature, which to the Deist was the chief evidence of God's existence; and it pleases the enlightened humanist by exalting man and giving him dominion over the earth, with no hint of conflict, sin, or punishment: 'And God saw everything that he had made, and, behold, it was very good.' Even Freemasons, Unitarians and Universalists could have no quarrel with this view.

It is not impossible that the author of the libretto was a Freemason. The modern masonic movement dates from the establishment of the Grand Lodge of England in 1717. Freemasons in England were not, as later on the Continent, associated with anticlericalism and revolution. In their theological position they did not differ greatly from moderate Deists: they emphasized the benevolence of the Creator (the Great Architect) as manifested in nature, but instead of attacking Christianity they upheld all monotheistic religions, and worked for international and interdenominational harmony.[10] The *Creation* libretto certainly tends in this direction, and possesses the calm dignity characteristic of masonic ritual. It is hard to detect in it any *specific* masonic symbolism, however.

In the parts inspired by Milton's *Paradise Lost*, the libretto is highly selective. No use is made of the long disputations between God and Satan; 'hell's spirits black' are dispatched to 'endless night' at an early stage (No. 2) and are heard from no more; there is only the briefest direct reference to the temptation and the Fall (No. 33). Milton is drawn on for lyrical detail in the descriptions of idyllic nature and of Adam and Eve's innocent love for each other. He is also the authority for God's motive in creating man, as expressed in No. 22; Milton put it thus:

> There wanted yet the Master work, the end
> Of all yet don; a Creature who not prone
> And Brute as other Creatures, but endu'd
> With Sanctitie of Reason, might erect
> His Stature, and upright with Front serene
> Govern the rest, self-knowing, and from thence
> Magnanimous to correspond with Heav'n,
> But grateful to acknowledge whence his good

Descends; thither with heart and voice and eyes
Directed in Devotion, to adore
And worship God Supream, who made him chief
Of all his works.[11]

This, as paraphrased in the second part of No. 22, can also be taken to justify the oratorio itself, in which choruses of praise form a large and prominent part; in particular, the Hymn of Adam and Eve (No. 30) can be seen as exemplifying precisely that praise for which God created man in his own image.

Politically, *The Creation* tends indirectly to support an enlightened State, neither on the one hand governed by sacerdotal or puritanical rigidity, nor on the other undermined by revolutionary extremes. The man, Adam, is depicted as holding power over material things, but as dutifully willing to subordinate that power to divine authority, and to guide his wife in the same sense. The woman, Eve, submits herself entirely to her husband: 'Thy will is law to me' (No. 31). The libretto does not go so far as Milton in female subjugation. For instance, Milton has Eve (but not Adam) say that all the beauties of creation are as nothing without her spouse,[12] while in *The Creation* both partners express this view (No. 32). So on this issue, which was hardly an explosive one in Georgian England, the libretto is mildly progressive.

It should be emphasized that the great majority of people were not concerned with theological disputes, which were conducted in learned and highly rationalistic terms, or even with high politics. But everybody knew and believed the creation story. If Handel had set this text to music, he could have been assured of the same broad popular acceptance from the English public that eventually greeted his other oratorios, and more especially *Messiah*. Handel, like many another composer of that age, searched out ways in which he could satisfy and communicate with his audience without sacrificing his own ideals and beliefs. Bred in a society dominated by patronage, it took him a long time to discover that in England the more important portion of that audience was the growing middle-class public. For that public the religious message of the Bible was a mainstay of their existence. It was this, far more than Handel's dramatic propensities, that brought his oratorios home to English hearts. And it was *Messiah*, portraying the central figure of religious life, that in the end sank deepest. *The Creation*, dealing with an equally basic, generalized theme, could well have joined it there. We do not know why Handel did not set the text: we do not know, even, whether it ever reached him. Fortunately another great master with a 'common touch' was able to take his place.

Religion in Catholic Austria

Liberal theology, including Deism, spread with other Enlightened modes of thought from England to France and America, and from France to Germany and Austria, though it was hardly welcomed by the Roman Catholic Church. An excellent study of the German intellectual and theological background to *The Creation* has been provided by Martin Stern.[13] His thesis assumes a far greater degree of originality in Swieten's contribution than the evidence will support. Nevertheless, for reasons stated above, the Austrian theological background must be regarded as relevant to the total context of the work and its reception.

Stern says that *The Creation* is the essence of the Enlightenment approach to religious feeling. He contrasts it with Bach's Passions, still bound by the old tradition of hatred of the flesh and consciousness of Adam's sin. The new philosophy, derived of course from the Greeks, showed much greater respect for the body, nature and natural virtue; the image of Adam was now cherished, while Bach had treated him as the cause of man's suffering. Gotthold Ephraim Lessing raged against the doctrine of the Fall; Gottfried Wilhelm Leibniz doubted the story of the Garden of Eden.[14]

Stern points out that *The Creation* embodies a new image and feeling for the world, with Light as the chief symbol of this consciousness. The worship of God is directly based on the beauty and reason of nature, a motive frequently repeated in the libretto;[15] Stern cites mid-eighteenth-century poems by Johann Peter Uz, Johann Adolf Schlegel and others that contain passages resembling Swieten's.[16]

These ideas were largely developed in northern, Protestant Germany, where there was an influence of English Deist and rationalist writers; they would have been strongly discouraged by the Roman Catholic hierarchy, and outlawed by the Austrian censor. However, Catholic Austria had experienced a species of liberal religion during the reign of Emperor Joseph II (1780–90). Motivated by the wish to diminish the political power of the Pope in his dominions, Joseph promulgated a series of decrees that virtually amounted to a Protestant reformation. 'Religion was to be purified from supersitition and meaningless ritual; religious instruction was to enlighten and generally improve the Christian citizen . . . the vernacular was introduced into the liturgy . . . . The desire for simplicity showed itself in decrees against excessive veneration of the Virgin, saints, and relics; altars and statues were to be reduced in number, as were processions and pilgrimages, candles and vestments.'[17]

Although these reforms were to be short-lived, they certainly introduced Austrians to a simpler, clearer and more rational kind of worship than their ancestors had known. Religion had been a mystery in the hands of priests; now it was brought into the light of day and shown to be related to common experience and to nature. Nevertheless, there is little to suggest that Deism made any headway in Vienna. Austrians did not have the freedom of speech that the English enjoyed, and an open dispute over the tenets of Christianity would not have been tolerated by Church or State, even under Joseph II.

The path for *The Creation* had been cleared by the earlier Viennese performance of German oratorios, and German translations of Handel's oratorios, which were associated of course with Protestantism and with relative freedom of theological position. Like them, it appealed over the heads of the Catholic Church to the people of Austria, by telling a story that was simple, attractive, and universally known and accepted. There was nothing in it that directly challenged official Christian teachings. Nevertheless, the Church quickly registered its objection to the work and banned it from sacred buildings,[18] presumably because of its associations, its secularity of thought and expression and its absence of emphasis on human sinfulness.

Some commentators have suggested that *The Creation* contains masonic musical symbolism:[19] Haydn was a Freemason, Swieten may have been one. This would certainly have increased the opposition of the Church and even the State. Freemasonry, after brief encouragement by Joseph II, had been made illegal in Austria in 1794. However, Haydn, unlike Mozart, has left no traces of continuing interest in masonry after his induction.[20] The generally humanistic flavour of the *Creation* text is certainly consistent with masonic ideas, as we have seen, but it has no specifically masonic ideas in it. The same is true of the music. The use of three parts, three angels and (sometimes) three flats or sharps is hardly striking enough to bear a message or symbol. To see what a composer might do to convey an explicit masonic message in music one has only to turn to *The Magic Flute*. Clearly Haydn was not following this example.

Haydn's religion

The composer's own religious orientation is believed to have been one of simple faith, but of an optimistic and tolerant kind not inconsistent with Enlightenment philosophy. Georg August Griesinger, whose biography is based on long conferences with Haydn during the composer's last years, has addressed this question:

Haydn was very religiously inclined, and was loyally devoted to the faith in which he was raised. He was very strongly convinced in his heart that all human destiny is under God's guiding hand, that God rewards good and evil, that all talents come from above ... [But he had no] intolerant feelings. Haydn left every man to his own conviction and recognized all as his brothers. In general, his devotion was not of the gloomy, always suffering sort, but rather cheerful and reconciled, and in this character, moreover, he wrote all his church music. His patriarchal, devout spirit is particularly expressed in *The Creation* ...[21]

Haydn habitually wrote 'Laus Deo' or 'Soli Deo gloria' at the end of his scores. In composing *The Creation* he evidently felt that he was performing a religious action. In response to a letter expressing admiration for the work, he wrote in 1802 '... A secret voice whispered to me: "There are in this world so few happy and contented people; sorrow and grief follow them everywhere; perhaps your labour will become a source in which the man bowed down by care, or burdened with business matters, will for a while find peace and rest." '[22]

Did Haydn, through his musical setting of this text, in any way modify its theological implications? If he did, it would seem to have been on his own initiative, since there is nothing in Swieten's written suggestions that has any bearing on theological matters.[23] It has been claimed by Siegmund Levarie[24] that Haydn placed a much greater emphasis on the Fall of Man than the text provides by the manner in which he wrote the last four numbers. Levarie sees the Fall expressed in two ways: first, 'the common-place conventionality of the musical substance of the second duet (No. 32) is a deliberate fall from the elevated level of the first duet (No. 30)'; second, a work that 'stands on C' as its principal key is made to end in B♭.

The question of key structure will be discussed in chapter 5. Here it may be pointed out, however, that Levarie's theory is hardly plausible from a theological standpoint. To be sure, the love music of Adam and Eve is less exalted than their hymn of praise, and draws much from opera; that is merely an appropriate response to the text. But this scene clearly occurs before the temptation and Fall, before even Uriel's warning of possible temptation (No. 33). To accept that Haydn deliberately built in symbolic references to the Fall – which Levarie traces back as far as No. 8, also in B♭ – we would have to believe that he was personally preoccupied with the doctrine of original sin, and was himself dissatisfied with a libretto that played down this aspect of the story. Such an assumption lacks plausibility, let alone evidence. To Levarie's question, 'Why did Haydn choose to conclude his oratorio as he did?' the short answer is, 'Because such an ending well suited both Haydn's inclinations and the text that had been supplied to him.'

The theological content of the oratorio, then, was well calculated to appeal to the ordinary Christian publics of both Austria and England. Its rationalistic, humanistic, naturalistic and optimistic approach to the creation also matched Enlightenment ideas. These ideas were advanced when the libretto was written and perhaps old-fashioned when the music was composed (as we shall see, it came under fire from some Romantic critics). But they happened to be well suited to Haydn's personal faith and temperament. Much credit is due to the sagacity of Salomon and Swieten for their respective parts in bringing this perfectly chosen text to the composer's attention.

3

The libretto

The Creation is the first large-scale work in musical history to be published with a bilingual text. It is clear from both the nature of the first edition, published by the composer himself, and the manner in which the work was composed, that Haydn intended to give equal standing to the German and English texts. This fact, which has only been fully understood in recent times, adds some complexity to the story of the work's composition.

Authorship

The original text of *The Creation* was English. No copy of it has been discovered, either in print or in manuscript. Gottfried van Swieten, who translated the libretto into German for Haydn, wrote the following about its origins at the end of December 1798:

My part in the work, which was originally in English, was certainly rather more than mere translation; but it was far from being such that I could regard it as *my own*. Neither is it by *Dryden* ... but by an unnamed author who had compiled it largely from *Milton's* Paradise Lost, and had intended it for Handel. What prevented the great man from making use of it is unknown; but when *Haydn* was in London it was looked out, and handed over to the latter with the request that he should set it to music.[1]

As Olleson points out, there are two other contemporary statements about the origin of the libretto. Griesinger, reporting Haydn's account, said: 'The first idea of the oratorio ... belongs to an Englishman, Lidley by name, and Haydn was to have composed Lidley's text for Salomon'; Albert Christoph Dies, another authentic contemporary source, stated that it was 'an already old text, in the English language' when Salomon handed it to Haydn in 1795.[2]

Thus it seems clear, on the balance of the evidence, that the original text had been written some fifty years earlier. Many writers have assumed that

Griesinger's 'Lidley' was really Thomas Linley the elder (1733–95), who was both old enough (if only just) to have written a libretto for Handel and long-lived enough to have offered it for Haydn's use. But Linley was no poet, and had no known connection with Handel. Olleson proposes the more plausible theory that the manuscript was among the Handel materials in the possession of John Christopher Smith, who took over the management of the oratorios from Handel, and whose successors in this position were his son (to whom he bequeathed the Handel manuscripts) and then Thomas Linley. Very probably the manuscript Salomon gave to Haydn came from Linley, and it was for that reason that his name was associated with it.

The candidacy of Mary Delany for authorship cannot be entertained, for although she did offer Handel a libretto based on *Paradise Lost*, it was concerned with the temptation and Fall, as was Benjamin Stillingfleet's book for John Christopher Smith's oratorio *Paradise Lost* (1760). Of the poets who provided librettos for Handel's existing oratorios, Olleson suggests Newburgh Hamilton as most likely, on the grounds that his text for *Samson* is based on Milton's *Samson Agonistes* in somewhat the same way that the *Creation* text is based on *Paradise Lost*. It must be said, however, that the literary level of *Samson* is more sophisticated that that of *The Creation*. Moreover the prosody of the two works is very different. While *Samson* uses regular blank-verse pentameters for recitative and rhyming strophic verse for arias, *The Creation* has prose for most recitatives and free unrhymed verse for arias and the remaining recitatives.

At present, then, we do not know who wrote the original text, nor is it at all probable that his or her identity will be established. But there is no reason to doubt that it was written for Handel. So the likely date range is 1733 to 1752; and thus it is primarily to early Georgian England that we must look for influences on its ideas and form.[3]

Sources, structure and revision

The original text was probably called *The Creation of the World*; this longer title survived in Salomon's first notice of his performance.[4] The author's principal sources were, first, the story of the creation as told in Genesis i.1 – ii.3 in the English translation of the Authorized (King James) Version of 1611; and second, the paraphrase, enrichment and interpretation of the same story in John Milton's *Paradise Lost* (revised version published 1674). A third source is the book of Psalms, especially xix. 1–5 (for Nos. 12 and 13) and civ. 27–30 (for No. 28).

Although we cannot examine the author's wordbook, we can deduce a good deal about its structure. As I have shown elsewhere,[5] the printed librettos offered for sale at Salomon's and John Ashley's London performances in 1800 contain traces of the original text. They support Olleson's contention that Swieten, far from writing a new libretto, closely followed the original, which he then translated into German, keeping as near as possible to the English word order and rhythm. In his own words, he 'resolved to clothe the English poem in German garb'. This will be discussed in more detail below.

Swieten did, however, make some changes. Again quoting his own account:

It is true that I followed the plan of the original faithfully as a whole, but I diverged from it in details as often as musical progress and expression, of which I already had an ideal conception in my mind, seemed to demand. Guided by these sentiments, I often judged it necessary that much should be shortened or even omitted, on the one hand, and on the other hand that much should be made more prominent or brought into greater relief, and much placed more in the shade.

We have no direct evidence of the extent of Swieten's structural alterations. Against his own account (which may have been distorted by his natural desire to claim as much credit as possible) there is the evidence of Princess Elenore Liechtenstein, who told her daughter on 1 May 1798 that Haydn was given an English poem and that Swieten had almost finished translating it 'without leaving anything out'.[6] However, there is, as we shall see, some internal evidence of structural changes.

The original text had considerable strength as a design for a large-scale muscial work. It fell into three Parts.[7] Part One covered the first four Days of Creation, Part Two the Fifth and Sixth Days, and Part Three dealt with Adam and Eve's gratitude and mutual love in the garden of Eden. Each Day was probably represented by a similar plan:

A. Prose from Genesis, in the past tense, for recitative.
B. Commentary in verse, in the present tense, for aria or ensemble.
C. Prose, in the past tense, for a recitative introducing ...
D. Choral hymn of praise by the heavenly host.

For the Third, Fifth and Sixth Days, A and B were recycled to allow for a second act of creation on the same Day; C and D then followed.

The librettist no doubt took the idea of C and D from *Paradise Lost*, Book IV:

> Thus was the first Day Eev'n and Morn:
> Nor past uncelebrated, nor unsung
> By the Celestial Quires ...
> with joy and shout
> The hollow Universal Orb they fill'd,
> And touch't their Golden Harps, & hymning prais'd
> God and his works, Creatour him they sung,
> Both when first Eevning was, and when first Morn.

And at the end of the Sixth Day:

> Up he rode
> Follow'd with acclamation and the sound
> Symphonious of ten thousand Harpes that tun'd
> Angelic harmonies: the Earth, the Aire
> Resounded ...[8]

In the *Creation* libretto as we have it (and as set out below, pp.52–64), traces of this idea survive at the end of every Day except the First. A and B are undisturbed, beginning at Nos. 1, 3, 5, 7, 11, 14, 16, 20 and 23. In each case, the concise biblical statement is followed by a lyrical, expansive paraphrase of the same act of creation. One early commentator considered that the aria texts had too much narrative in them, especially since, in an aria, words are generally repeated many times.[9]

C is seen clearly in Nos. 9, 12 (last two lines), 17 and 25 (second sentence). In each of these the language is in the style of bibilical prose, with an echo of Milton in No. 17; each passage was surely designed for recitative introducing a chorus of praise. But No. 17 is displaced (by Swieten, no doubt), occurring before B, the angels' commentary on the preceding act of creation (18), instead of before D, the chorus of praise (19). Nos. 10, 13, 19 and 26/28 are clear examples of D.

At the end of the First Day there is no sign of either C or D, and it seems a reasonable inference that such movements were once present but were eliminated or used elsewhere by Swieten, perhaps to counterbalance his idea (an inspired one, as it turned out) of interpolating choruses in the two opening movements. At the end of the Second Day, No. 4 has subject matter similar to C (as in 9 or 17, for instance), but it is in the free iambic verse otherwise reserved for angels' commentary, and is set as an aria rather than a recitative. The chorus, instead of voicing praise, repeats this narrative statement made by Gabriel. It seems likely that Swieten made a large-scale change here; there is evidence that this movement underwent several textual revisions.[10]

The chorus sings narrative in No. 1 only, commentary in Nos. 2 and 4 only. If, as seems probable, each of these instances was due to Swieten, we can see that the original author's plan was to have the chorus consistently representing the heavenly host praising God for his works. No. 27 fits rather awkwardly into the scheme. The original author may have seen fit to expand the angels' praise after the Sixth Day by stressing creation's subservience to God at this point; another possibility is that this section was originally in Part Three, and was moved to its present place by Swieten.

To whom were the solos assigned in the original libretto? In this case we have no source more authentic than Swieten's manuscript text,[11] for the London librettos reflect the later decisions. In Swieten's text the recitatives are assigned to 'Ein Engel', which may be a translation from the English original (the introduction of three named angels was a later development), while the arias are merely assigned to soprano, tenor or bass. The English author's intention may well have been to give all the narrative prose texts (A and C) to a single 'narrator' angel, while commentary (B), in the present tense, could be sung by various voices, representing the heavenly host actually witnessing the scene. However, Swieten assigned most recitative/aria pairs to the same voice type, and later to a named angel. Perhaps Haydn liked this arrangement; it conforms to the operatic *scena*. But the result is that the same singer has to shift from past to present tense, with an illogical and sometimes confusing effect.

Other probable cases of Swieten's often clumsy intervention are revealed by changes of style and even faulty grammar in the middle of a movement. In No. 12, as already mentioned, two lines of prose narrative are tacked on to a nine-line lyric, with an unjustified change from present to past tense; similarly in No. 22. In No. 2 a past tense, 'fled', occurs in the middle of a passage in the present. In No. 4 the plural verb 'resound' has a singular subject, 'praise'. In the Trio, No. 18, the first verse, sung by Gabriel, seems out of place, as it would belong more logically to the Third Day; one may suspect the hand of Swieten here, since everywhere else the angels' commentary faithfully reflects the preceding biblical narrative.

Part Three of the libretto departs altogether from the biblical account. The recitatives are now in free iambic verse. Adam and Eve come on the scene, to sing first a Hymn that recounts once again the major works of Creation, and then a love duet; both are inspired by Milton.[12] After the brief warning not to succumb to temptation, there is a final chorus of praise by the heavenly host. No evidence exists of structural alterations in this part of the work. (However, in the first eight lines of No. 32 the use of the gender-neutral words 'consort' and 'spouse' strongly suggests that the original intention was for a duet in which both Adam and Eve sang all the words, perhaps in the traditional two-verse form designed for a da capo).

We can gather from these indications some idea of the type of structural changes Swieten made in the libretto: he confessed to having 'shortened, or even omitted' material, and to having changed the emphasis placed on different parts. If my analysis is correct, his alterations show scant respect for the overall design. His German translation has survived with his annotations,[13] and we can see that in some cases the composer adopted his suggestions. Thus, although we are free to criticize Swieten for butchering the author's admirable plan, we must also give him credit for the ultimately more important achievement of providing Haydn with a text that generated one of the greatest of all oratorios.

It is well to bear in mind also that Haydn may have played a part in the textual revisions. Frederik Samuel Silverstolpe, a Swedish diplomat who was close to Haydn during the composition of the oratorio, reports that Haydn said to him: 'I find it necessary to confer often with the Baron, to make changes in the text...'[14] We do not know whether these conferences preceded or followed the surviving manuscript of Swieten's text.

Literary character

The style of the libretto has come under relentless attack, particularly in England, almost from the beginning (see pp. 44, 95). We may grant that the overall plan was well conceived, but the details are less happy. Despite the influence of two of the greatest works of English literature, the King James Bible and *Paradise Lost*, it is clear that the unknown author's poetic technique and imagination fell a long way short of the exalted subject he had chosen.

It is in the airs, ensembles and choruses that the librettist was called on to provide lyrical expression. He chose an unconventional and not in itself unattractive style of verse: iambics, with unrhymed lines of varying length. (The chief exceptions are the Hymn, No. 30, which has a regular structure of 'common metre' strophes, with choral answers in four-foot iambics; and the first part of the Duet, No. 32, which is trochaic.) He allowed himself a good deal of freedom, following English rather than Italian precedent, in varying the stresses and even adding extra syllables. The general rhythm and tone, as well as many of the ideas, are Miltonian.

But unfortunately the choice of epithets is often inept or even bizarre: 'holy beams', 'outrageous storms', 'dreary, wasteful hail', 'closèd wood', 'expanded boughs', 'flexible[15] tyger', 'cumb'rous elements'. The model was probably Milton, who was the direct source of some other unusual phrases ('serpent error', 'sinuous trace'), but the imitator altogether lacked the master's touch. He has 'See flashing through the wet / In throngèd swarms the fry / On thousand ways around' where Milton had 'Forthwith the Sounds and Seas, each Creek and Bay / With Frie innumerable swarme, and Shoales / Of Fish that with their Finns and shining Scales / Glide under the green Wave'.[16]

When the author allowed his own imagination and humour some scope, the results sometimes border on the ridiculous, as when the sun is called 'an am'rous, joyful, happy spouse' (No. 12), or days and nights are made to talk to each other (No. 13): both passages are travesties of Psalm xix ('the sun, Which is as a bridegroom coming out of his chamber, and rejoiceth as a strong man to run a race'; 'Day unto day uttereth speech, and night unto night sheweth knowledge'). Again, the word-order inversion frequently so delightful in Milton becomes awkward in the hands of his disciple ('Him celebrate, him magnify!', 'How grateful is Of fruits the savour sweet') and in some cases an obstacle to understanding ('The marv'lous work beholds amazed The glorious hierarchy of heav'n'; 'The wonder of his works Displays the firmament'). To be fair, it should be said that some of the oddities of the final English text may have originated with Swieten or even Haydn. As we will see below, they had practical reasons to alter it and did, in fact, do so in some spots.

However, it is a fatal mistake to judge a libretto simply as poetry. It is not meant to be read (although some librettists such as Metastasio may have had a reader in mind more than a listener). Notoriously, many of the greatest operas and oratorios have librettos not only without poetic merit but incapable of rational interpretation. Some, such as *The Magic Flute* and *Il trovatore*, make *The Creation* look like a model of clarity.

The *Creation* libretto has all the essentials of a good oratorio text. It avoids theological or philosophical exposition, which tends to inhibit musical expression. It has a clear and familiar 'plot', with a narrative not unsuited to declamatory recitative. And it has an abundance of lyrical verse rich in imagery. The many pictorial descriptions happened to suit Haydn well, and Salomon may have chosen this work for that reason, knowing how strongly Haydn had been impressed by *Israel in Egypt*. Another feature that was not lost on Haydn was the humour, both intentional and otherwise, that is to be found here and there in the text.

The chief drawback is the almost complete absence of dramatic conflict. Indeed, only No. 2, No. 3 (the 'outrageous storms') and No. 27 (Raphael's verse) contain any extended treatment of evil or negative material. But the theory that oratorio is necessarily a dramatic form cannot be sustained by historical evidence.[17] A large part of the function of oratorio has always been to provide formal and emotional support for, and reinvigoration of, the religious beliefs and moral self-confidence of a society. The *Creation* libretto, whatever its weakness of verbal detail, was admirably suited to that function. Its ultimate justification is that it provided material for Haydn's greatest work, and, enriched by his music, continues to stimulate and move audiences around the world.

Translation and adaptation

Swieten, as already mentioned, said that he 'resolved to clothe the poem in German garb'. How literally this was true was first revealed by Edward Olleson in his 1968 article, subsequently reinforced by my own work.[18] Swieten's function was not, as previously thought, simply that of providing a German text for Haydn to set to music. Since the oratorio was designed for London as well as Vienna, Swieten had the much more difficult and possibly unprecedented task of giving Haydn a *bilingual* text.

Haydn evidently had the ambition not only of crowning his Austrian career, but of taking his place in the great English oratorio tradition headed by Handel. Yet his knowledge of English was very limited; he had to have a German text to stimulate his musical ideas. Swieten, therefore, set himself the task of writing a German text that would come as close as possible to the English libretto as he had now revised it.

The clearest indication that this was his procedure is in the biblical recitatives. With trivial exceptions the English text of these is identical in wording to the version in the King James Bible, whereas the German text corresponds to no known German Bible translation.[19] Instead, it is so constructed that the word order, syllabification and stress patterns are as close as possible to the English. Haydn and Swieten must have realized that English audiences would not easily accept changes in the hallowed text of their Bible; and there were the formidable precedents of *Messiah* and *Israel in Egypt* to bear in mind.

In the non-biblical passages Swieten pursued the same objective – to create a bilingual text for simultaneous setting. But here he must have felt he could take a freer hand with the English text. If he found a German phrase to his liking, the English could be altered to conform to it. There are, indeed, a number of cases where he did just that, as we can tell by comparing the English text in the first edition of the full score (provided for Haydn by Swieten) with that in Salomon's and Ashley's printed librettos. For instance in No. 30 the English printed librettos, and presumably the original English text, had the line 'This world, so wondrous and so great'. Swieten translated this 'Die Welt, so gross, so wunderbar' and then altered the English to 'This world, so great, so wonderful'.[20] Presumably he could not find a German translation that matched the original English phrase in rhythm and structure; but it was equally efficacious to do the reverse, so long as Haydn could be presented with a German text which, when set to music, could be replaced by the English.

It must be said that Swieten accomplished this daunting task with considerable skill. Translations for singing are difficult enough to achieve even after the music has been composed, and always involve some compromise or sacrifice either of sense or of rhythm. To accomplish such a thing perfectly before composition was a practical impossibility, for Swieten could not know precisely what elements of the text Haydn would single out for emphasis, repetition, or contrapuntal exchange. Moreover, perfect command of both languages would have been needed to carry out the task at all well, and this Swieten did not have. For instance, he treated 'eagle' and 'cattle' as one syllable each, 'glides' as two, and 'stately' as three, and was satisfied with such nonsense as this:

> O happy pair, and always happy yet,
> If not, misled by false conceit,
> Ye strive at more, as granted is,
> And more to know, as know ye should!

Clearly, in lines 3 and 4 the original 'than' was twice translated 'als' and then mistranslated back to 'as', while 'if not' should read 'unless'.

As a German libretto, Swieten's translation must be pronounced an unqualified success. We cannot doubt that Haydn was delighted with it and found that it stimulated him to unparalleled creative accomplishment. It at once captivated the Viennese audiences, and later the wider public of all German-speaking lands. It is true that the libretto, considered as a German poem, was heavily criticised as inadequate from the first: Schiller called it a 'charakterloser Mischmasch'.[21] But as a vehicle for Haydn's music it has been rather consistently admired. Max Friedländer considered Swieten 'among the most discerning advisors and cleverest librettists ... that a composer ever found', and a still higher evaluation has been offered by Martin Stern (who, however, was under the impression that Swieten largely created the text).[22]

Regardless of the precise degree of originality in Swieten's German text, then, he succeeded in striking exactly the right note for the purpose. The choruses suggest the extrovert grandeur of Handel, who was becoming widely known on the Continent. The biblical and Miltonian passages preserve something of their epic quality in literal translation; for, after all, the two languages are cousins, a fact which may be more obvious in poetry than in academic prose. The naïveté of the pictorial passages also comes across well in German, while the oddity of some of the wording is less glaring, probably because of Swieten's greater skill in his own tongue. Finally, grammatical ambiguity resulting from word-order inversions is not a problem, since the German case-endings generally remove it; apart from some inconsistencies of tense, most of the grammatical anomalies mentioned above disappear in the German version. In all these ways the German text is smoother and more conventional than the English.

After Haydn had finished composing the work, and probably after the early Viennese performances, Swieten had an additional task: he had to underlay the English text in preparation for the bilingual edition. He carried out this assignment in one of the manuscript copies of the full score made by Johann Elssler and an assistant. This document has survived (Berlin, Stiftung Preussischer Kulturbesitz, Mus.ms.9851). In solos, including recitatives, Swieten wrote the desired English text above the voice part (the German text being below), and he did the same for the soprano part in the choruses. At many points, especially in the recitatives, he provided alternative musical readings in small notes to make a better fit with the English text rhythm; for, of course, the rhythms of the two texts were not exactly the same, despite his earlier efforts.

In half a dozen cases Swieten found that the English text could not be made to fit Haydn's music, because of the way Haydn had divided or repeated a German phrase. For instance in No. 30, bars 82–5, the original English text was 'In your extended course proclaim'; Swieten had translated this 'Macht kund auf eurer weiten Bahn', which correctly preserved both the meaning and rhythm of the English. But Haydn in his setting gave special emphasis to the phrase 'Macht kund', repeating it in some parts.

Swieten saw that 'In your' could not be treated in the same way, so he adroitly reordered the English text: 'Proclaim in your extended course.' The process can be clearly seen in the manuscript.[23]

But there were far more places where Swieten made no attempt to fit the English text to the music. Generally speaking, there was not enough room to insert the English for the lower chorus parts; where they differ in rhythm from the soprano part, it is often unclear how the words are to be fitted. Again, in the many passages where the German text is repeated in the course of a movement, Swieten generally failed to repeat the English text.

The first edition of the full score is in these respects a close copy of Berlin Mus.ms.9851. Thus it provided a rough guide for an English-language performance. The intention was clear, and was emphasized by a double title page: the top half in German, the lower half in English (see p. 37; the two halves were reversed in a later Breitkopf & Härtel reissue[24]). But the execution was utterly inadequate. In the first place, Swieten's effort to adapt the music, especially in the recitatives, produced some unnatural stresses, such as those in Ex. 1 ('firmament' needs an accent on the first syllable; 'thine', not 'am', is the emphatic word in (b)). More seriously, there

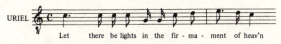

Let there be lights in the fir - ma - ment of heav'n

Example 1 (a) No. 11 (Recitative), bars 2–3

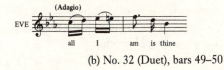

all I am is thine

(b) No. 32 (Duet), bars 49–50

are many problems in the lower chorus parts and in passages of repeated text, with no attempt to provide a solution. To take a simple example, in Ex. 2 it is by no means clear what words the lower voices are to sing; there is an extra syllable to fit in, and no indication of how to do it.

Thus the score raises literally hundreds of problems for anyone wishing to use it for an English-language performance. This might well have defeated the purpose of the exercise; but, as we shall see, successful performances did take place in England. What seems likely is that the inadequacy of Swieten's adaptation, rather than of the text itself, was the

Example 2 No. 1, chorus entry (bars 76–80), as in the first edition

prime cause of the low reputation that the libretto soon acquired in Great Britain, prompting the long series of revisions in the text and word underlay that was made in subsequent English editions.

Swieten cannot be blamed for his imperfect understanding of English (more fully revealed in his translation of his own libretto for *The Seasons*). But he could surely have consulted a native speaker who was also a musician; and he could, in any case, have done his adaptation more thoroughly, seeing to the repetitions and lower voice parts. It may well be that he was far less interested than Haydn in the oratorio's English future, and carried out this part of his work in a perfunctory fashion. He said, indeed, that it was 'in order that the Fatherland might be the first to enjoy it [the composition]' that he had 'resolved to clothe the English poem in German garb'. Clearly that was the principal and by far the most successful part of his contribution: the German, not the English text.

4

Composition, performance and reception

Genesis and composition

It is not known exactly when Salomon handed the *Creation* libretto to Haydn and asked him to set it to music, but according to Swieten 'he was just on the point of leaving for Vienna', which he did on 15 August 1795 at the end of his second visit to London. One account claims that it was not Salomon but François Hippolyte Barthélemon (1741–1808), the French violinist and composer resident in London, who first suggested the idea:

During Haydn's stay in England he was so much struck with the performance of Handel's 'Messiah', that he intimated to his friend Barthelemon his great desire to compose a work of a similar kind. He asked Barthelemon what subject he would advise for such a purpose. Barthelemon took up his Bible and said, 'There, take that, and begin at the beginning!' Barthelemon assured my father that this was the origin of the idea of the composition of 'The Creation'.[1]

But whether the idea was Barthélemon's or Salomon's, it was the latter who actually provided the text. Swieten says:

At first sight the material seemed to him [Haydn] indeed well chosen, and well suited to musical effects, but he nevertheless did not accept the proposal immediately; he was just on the point of leaving for Vienna, and he reserved the right to announce his decision from there, where he wanted to take a look at the poem. [On his return] he then showed it to me ... I recognized at once that such an exalted subject would give Haydn the opportunity I had long desired, to show the whole compass of his profound accomplishments and to express the full power of his inexhaustible genius; I therefore encouraged him to take the work in hand...[2]

After his return to Vienna Haydn began to give thought to the subject. At first he was occupied with other music: piano trios, masses, string quartets and the choral version of *The Seven Last Words*. The first direct reference to *The Creation* is in a letter of 15 December 1796 from Johann Georg

Albrechtsberger to Beethoven: 'Yesterday Haydn came to me, he is carrying round in his head the idea of a big oratorio which he intends to call "The Creation" and hopes to finish it soon. He improvised some of it for me and I think it will be very good.'[3] Neither Swieten nor the sources derived from Haydn himself (Dies and Griesinger) tell us just when Swieten revised and translated the text for Haydn, nor at what point the Gesellschaft der Associierten definitely commissioned the work for performance in the spring of 1798.

The surviving manuscript libretto prepared for Haydn by Swieten is annotated with a number of hints for the composer's benefit. To us it may seem that he was presumptuous to offer such advice to the most famous living composer. But in Haydn's day it was not unusual for a librettist to dictate such details, and Swieten had the added authority of rank. In fact several of his suggestions were adopted by the composer (they are set out in detail, and compared with Haydn's actual procedure, by H. C. Robbins Landon[4]). Moreover, according to one account Swieten 'had each piece, as soon as it was ready, copied and pre-rehearsed with a small orchestra. Much he discarded as too trivial [*kleinlich*] for the grand subject. Haydn gladly submitted [*fügte sich*] ... '[5] We are bound to conclude that Swieten's judgment was a factor of considerable significance in many of Haydn's decisions regarding *The Creation*.

The main work of composition took place during the year 1797. In March or April of that year Haydn played the Introduction, 'Representation of Chaos', to Silverstolpe, and commented: 'You have certainly noticed how I avoided the resolutions that you would most readily expect. The reason is, that there is no form in anything [in the universe] yet.' In the early summer he showed Silverstolpe No. 6: 'You see,' he said in joking tone, 'you see how the notes run up and down like the waves; see there, too, the mountains that come from the depths of the sea? One has to have some amusement after one has been serious for so long.' We rely chiefly on Silverstolpe for the knowledge that Haydn completed the first draft of *The Creation* at Eisenstadt in the autumn of 1797.[6]

It is clear that Haydn worked primarily with the German text during the process of composition, and this is borne out both by the surviving sketches and by the fact that Swieten had to adapt the English text to fit the music afterwards. Yet there are a few passages that seem strikingly to match the English better than the German, and lead one to suppose that Haydn did keep the English text in mind as well.[7]

The quantity of surviving sketches for *The Creation* is unique in Haydn's career, according to Landon.[8] There are no less than seven sketches for 'Chaos', five for No. 30, three each for Nos. 10 and 13, and one or two for each of fourteen other movements. As these have not yet been precisely dated, they do not provide concrete assistance in determining the timetable of composition and revision. A partial analysis of the sketches, with full transcription of many of them, has been provided by Landon.[9]

With a handful of exceptions, it appears from these sketches that Haydn rarely made radical changes in his material once he had conceived it and put it on paper. We do learn of a few changes of mind. The great chorus 'The heavens are telling' (No. 13) was originally to be in D major.[10] Raphael's recitative 'Be fruitful, and multiply' (No. 16, bars 6–22) was at first provided with a 'bare accompaniment of the bass moving solemnly in a steady rhythm', following Swieten's suggestion,[11] and this idea survives in the earliest score, where the bass is written for cello and double bass *senza cembalo*; later the two solo cello parts were added above, and still later the two violas as well, creating the rich texture known to us in the final version.[12] An early idea for the 'bird' aria, 'On mighty pens' (No. 15), is in triple time, but is still recognizably the same melody (see Ex. 3)[13].

(On mighty pens uplifted soars the eagle aloft)

Example 3 Sketch for No. 15

One sketch that was entirely rejected was the first draft for the Hymn (No. 30). It seems that Haydn's original plan was for a duet movement, 'By thee with bliss', followed by a separate chorus, 'For ever blessed be his power'; the two sets of words appear successively in all versions of the libretto. Only later did he conceive the idea of having them sung simultaneously. The rejected chorus is set out with modern clefs by Landon.[14] Ex. 4 shows a portion of it that became, instead, the basis for parts of the Trio, No. 27 (bars 35–8, 60–3).

(His name be ever magnified)

Example 4 Sketch for No. 30

The seven surviving sketches for the 'Chaos' reveal the unusual amount of creative energy Haydn expended on this movement. The one that Landon identifies as the earliest[15] already indicates the successive suspensions, the triplet phrases from different parts of the orchestra, and the extraordinary sequence of harmonies in bars 5–15, but it is apparent that Haydn then intended to move to a conventional cadence in E♭: only later did he decide to delay that cadence indefinitely. The next in chronological sequence is an outline beginning with the great unison C and extending to bar 26, but still without the haunting opening violin phrase (bars 3–5), which has a later sketch to itself. By the time of the fourth sketch, the movement is complete in all essentials, but there was evidently a long further process of working out details before the composer was satisfied.[16]

First performances in Vienna

Under the supervision of Johann Elssler, Haydn's chief copyist, several copies of the score and parts[17] were made in the early months of 1798, and on 6 April Prince Joseph zu Schwarzenberg was informed that the work was ready for performance. All the rehearsals and performances of this first season were given at the Palais Schwarzenberg, Vienna. Silverstolpe described a rehearsal that took place a few days before the first performance:

Prince Schwarzenberg . . . was so utterly enchanted by the many beauties of the work that he presented the composer with a roll containing one hundred ducats, over and above the 500 that were part of the agreement. – No one, not even Baron van Swieten, had seen the page of the score wherein the birth of light is described. That was the only passage of the work which Haydn had kept hidden. I think I see his face even now, as this part sounded in the orchestra. Haydn had the expression of someone who is thinking of biting his lips, either to conceal his embarrassment (*Verlegenheit*) or to conceal a secret. And in that moment when light broke out for the first time, one would have said that rays darted from the composer's burning eyes.[18]

An open rehearsal took place on 29 April and the official first performance on 30 April. The three soloists were Christine Gerardi, Mathias Rathmayer and Ignaz Saal; Antonio Salieri played piano continuo and Haydn himself directed. A number of first-hand accounts bear witness to the ecstatic reception and the furore that followed in Viennese aristocratic circles.[19] Because of the enormous demand, two additional performances were given on 7 and 10 May.

These early performances were, however, exclusive and semi-private in nature. The larger Viennese public had to wait until the following year for an opportunity to hear the great work. The delay may have been due to threats of legal action by Salomon, referred to by Griesinger[20] and also mentioned in the Viennese press at the time.[21] After two more private performances at the Palais Schwarzenberg on 2 and 4 March, the first public performance was given at the Burgtheater on 19 March 1799. A poster advertising the performance included a request to the audience, in the composer's name, to refrain from demanding encores of individual numbers.[22]

This time the performance was on a grander 'public' scale, though still small by comparison with the Handel Festival which Haydn had witnessed in 1791. The most reliable accounts suggest that about 180 performers took part, as in all Haydn's full-scale performances of the work: probably about 120 players and 60 singers (men and boys).[23] It was on this occasion also, no doubt, that Haydn introduced the additional parts for bass trombone and contrabassoon and tripled the wind parts, as shown in some of the early sources.[24] An additional excitement was the debut of the attractive seventeen-year-old soprano Therese Saal, who replaced Gerardi as Gabriel/Eve. At the piano was Kapellmeister Joseph Weigl; Haydn directed as before, and at the end was called forward to tumultuous applause, in which the Emperor joined. The success of this performance was stupendous, indeed rarely equalled in the history of music.[25] The next public performance was on 22 December, again at the Burgtheater, and was given by the composer for the benefit of the Widows and Orphans Fund of the Tonkünstler-Societät.

After this time performances of the work in Lent and Advent became a regular part of Vienna's musical life. Haydn conducted many of them himself until the end of 1802. His last appearance in public was the famous occasion on 27 March 1808, when a small-scale performance (in Italian, with about 32 singers and 60 players) was given at the University of Vienna in honour of his 76th birthday. Haydn had been infirm for some years, and had to be brought in in a chair. At the words 'And there was light', thunderous applause interrupted the performance. It was almost exactly ten years since Haydn had first heard this stunning passage. The old man, 'the tears streaming down his pallid cheeks and as if overcome by the most violent emotions, raised his trembling arms to heaven, as if in prayer to the Father of Harmony'.[26]

Publication

In June 1799 Haydn announced in several journals that he would himself publish the full score of *The Creation*, with German and English texts, and he invited subscriptions.[27] After a number of postponements it appeared late in February 1800, and was advertised in Viennese newspapers on 1 March.[28] The title page is reproduced in Figure 1. Next followed the list of subscribers. An amplified version of this list exists in Haydn's handwriting, showing that he himself supervised the details of publication; it has been printed by Landon.[29]

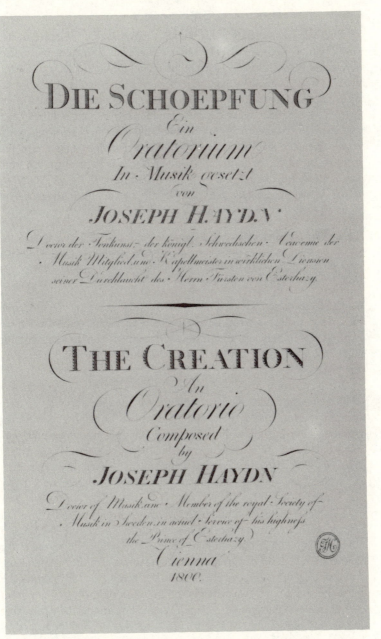

Figure 1 Title page of the first edition of *Die Schöpfung / The Creation*

The engraver's copy for this edition survives in the Gesellschaft der Musikfreunde, Vienna (MS. H 27405).[30] It is a fair copy made by Elssler, with words in German and English; the model for both texts, and for the alternate musical readings to go with them, was almost certainly the Berlin manuscript already referred to, in which the English text had been added by Swieten, with certain minor alterations in the German text and the music, most in Swieten's hand, a few in Haydn's.[31] It is clear that Haydn took great trouble to ensure that the printed score accurately reflected his considered decisions on all details of the music and texts. It was precisely in this form that he wished his oratorio to be disseminated through the world and so passed on to posterity. His motives are clearly stated in the announcement of the edition:

The work is to appear in full score, so that on the one hand, the public may have the work in its entirety, and so that the connoisseur may see it *in toto* and thus better judge it; while on the other, it will be easier to prepare the parts, should one wish to perform it anywhere.[32]

With such authority, we need not go beyond this score for the authentic musical text, except to justify the correction of accidental errors (which are relatively few in number) or to resolve ambiguities. Any later additions or alterations made by the composer were designed for local and temporary circumstances.

A. Peter Brown has made a comprehensive study of several manuscript scores and sets of parts which were used at some large-scale Viennese performances under the composer's direction or with his approval. They include additional scoring (for bass trombone and contrabassoon), and differentiation of wind parts between *solo* and *tutti* passages. They also show vocal embellishments and marks of dynamics and articulation which are illuminating as guides for performance today (see Appendix 1).[33]

The plates of the first edition were sold to Breitkopf and Härtel, of Leipzig, who published two later issues, the earlier dating from 1803. Erard and Pleyel issued full scores in Paris shortly after 1800. There were also a number of reductions and arrangements, and prints of individual numbers, demonstrating the enormous popularity of the work in the early years of the nineteenth century.[34] Two reductions have some authority deriving from their nearness to the composer: Anton Wranitzky's arrangement for string quintet, and Sigismund Neukomm's piano/vocal score, both published by Artaria a short time after the full score appeared. Muzio Clementi's piano/vocal score, published in London probably in the summer of 1800, is important as the first attempt to deal with the problems presented by Swieten's failure to reconcile the English text with the music.

Once the full score had been issued, *The Creation* became available as public property, and performances quickly followed in many German cities and foreign capitals. Early vocal scores and librettos with French and Italian texts show the spreading demand for the work. There also began a steady stream of English-language editions, reductions and arrangements that have continued uninterruptedly to the present day.

By the time of Haydn's death in 1809 there were at least four piano-vocal scores in print, as well as a score for piano solo (in an arrangement by Carl Czerny), three arrangements for string quintet or quartet, and many editions of individual numbers. In course of time various numbers would be used as the basis for anthems, hymns, and pieces for piano and organ. Perhaps the greatest curiosity was a set of sonatas freely based on themes from *The Creation*, which was composed by the famous pianist Joseph Wölfl (1773–1812) and published in 1801.[35] They are skilful and surprisingly effective pieces, and the twenty-seven themes are numbered with reference to a key that supplies the original texts.

First London performances

In London Salomon had hoped to be able to present the first English performance at the Oratorio Concert he directed at the King's Theatre, Haymarket, and had subscribed to twelve copies of the full score for this purpose. But his plan was thwarted by a rival impresario, John Ashley, who managed to 'scoop' the London premiere at the Covent Garden Oratorio on 28 March. According to an authentic account, Ashley's copy of the printed score had reached him 'on Saturday, 22 March ... at nine o'clock in the evening, by a King's messenger from Vienna; was copied into parts by Mr. Thomas Goodwin for 120 performers; rehearsed, and performed at Covent Garden on the Friday following.'[36] More than simple copying was involved. The English text is not fully underlaid in the printed full score, and a number of other problems would have been encountered in adapting the music to the English text.

Salomon had to be content with the fourth London performance, on 21 April. In a public exchange with Ashley, he claimed that he 'had been favoured, exclusively, by Dr. HAYDN with particular directions on the stile and manner in which [the oratorio] ought to be executed, to produce the effects required by the Author'.[37] If this was anything more than a mere advertising puff, the 'directions' have never been found.

The number of performers quoted above, 120, shows that these London performances were not on so large a scale as Haydn's at Vienna (let alone the great Handel Commemoration, which in 1791 had enrolled over a thousand performers). The dimensions were the normal ones for the annual Lent Oratorio season. Between the parts of the work, concertos were performed, as was customary. A curious feature is that both Ashley and Salomon employed more vocal soloists than the score demands.[38]

Of the two performances Salomon's boasted the more famous names. He secured Gertrude Mara, the leading soprano in London, as well as Sophia Dussek; the two ladies appear to have shared the parts of both Gabriel and Eve, judging by contemporary sheet music editions of individual songs in which their names are mentioned. Salomon's leading bass was James Bartleman and his tenor John Page. Ashley announced no less than nine soloists, of which the best known were Mary Second (née Mahon) and Charles Incledon. One bass singer, a Mr Denman, took part in both productions.

The Creation was received with measured enthusiasm by the English press.[39] The opinion was quickly formed that it was inferior to Handel's oratorios. As early as 1802 it became quite usual to perform only the first part of the work in England,[40] culminating in 'The heavens are telling', which was regarded by the English as the most sublime movement of the whole oratorio. Full acceptance of the work by the British public seems to date from Sir George Smart's performance at Drury Lane Theatre on 17 March 1813, 'when, in order to render it more attractive, and perhaps more interesting, in the undeveloped state of musical taste at the time, it was interspersed with Recitations from Milton's *Paradise Lost*, by the favourite tragic actress, Miss Smith [later Mrs Bartley]'.[41] It then entered the standard repertory of provincial choral festivals (such as those at Norwich, from 1813; Edinburgh, 1815; and York, 1823) – the only non-Handel work to do so until Spohr's *Last Judgement* in the 1830s.

Early Paris performances

The Creation was introduced to France under very different conditions, during the turmoil of war and at a time when Napoleon as First Consul was engaged in consolidating his power over the restless French people. Indeed, Ignace Pleyel's plan to bring Haydn to conduct the work at the

Opéra in August 1800 was frustrated by his inability to gain entry to France. The actual first performance was at the Théâtre des Arts on 24 December 1800; Napoleon, on the way to the performance in his carriage, only just escaped assassination by a bomb concealed in a street water cart.[42] The news tended to distract the audience of 1417 persons from the music, and the performance was financially a disaster. Nevertheless, according to contemporary accounts, it was received with acclamation. There were reportedly 250 performers on this occasion; the in-house conductor, Jean-Baptiste Rey, directed the performance; at the piano was Daniel Steibelt, the Prussian pianist-composer who was temporarily in the French capital.

The version used at this and other early French performances was far from authentic. The text was translated into prose by Steibelt, and then put into bad French verse by one Joseph Ségur. According to contemporary reviews, Steibelt changed the keys of many movements (the part of Adam was rewritten for a 'mezzo tenore', P.J. Garat), altered various passages, omitted the love duet (No. 32) and added to the orchestration.[43] The published full score of Steibelt's version[44] does not show these changes, but it cuts out the final chorus, ending with a recitative (No. 33). The piano-vocal score based on this edition makes it clear that the intention was to end by repeating No. 28 at the end of Part Three; why this was preferred to No. 34 is not easy to see.

A second performance took place on 1 January 1801, and there were many more in succeeding years; Haydn's popularity overcame the political hostilities between France and Austria. In the view of the Paris correspondents of German periodicals,[45] this was a highly significant event in French musical life: according to one, it was 'as much a triumph for France as for the fatherland of this immortal artist. Great men belong to the nations who know how to appreciate them.'[46] As was customary with all important new productions, *The Creation* was rapidly followed by a parody at a vaudeville theatre, entitled *La récréation du monde, suite de l'oratorio: la création du monde, musique d'Haydn en vaudeville*.[47] Unfortunately the score of this interesting travesty does not seem to be extant.

First American performances

Some numbers from *The Creation* appeared in American publications early in the new century, but the first performance of the work is believed to have been a partial one put on by the Moravians at Bethlehem, Pennsylvania, in

1810.[48] This would have been in German. The score was copied, presumably from the first edition, by Johann Friedrich Peter, and is preserved at the Moravian Music Foundation in Winston-Salem, North Carolina.

The Boston Handel and Haydn Society, founded in 1815, presented selections from Part One in English at Stone Chapel, Boston, on Christmas Day of that year; the coupling of Haydn's name with Handel's in this august choral society seems to have been entirely due to *The Creation*. The three parts were offered on separate days in April 1817, and a complete performance in English was given at Boylston Hall, Boston, on 16 February 1819.[49] Frequent performances followed in New York and many other cities.[50]

Later Thomas Hastings, in the second edition of his influential *Dissertation on Musical Taste*, wrote as follows:

Haydn's 'Creation', as well as Handel's 'Messiah', has been extensively admired in this country, and it continues to be performed in many places, now after the lapse of some thirty years, almost with undiminished interest. True, it has faults. It has its harmonic crudities: it has some odd fancies, and questionable traits of description; and here and there may be traced an abortive specimen of the imitative. But what work is perfect? Haydn's music is too enchanting to have anything to fear from criticism.[51]

Critical reception

The Creation has proved to be one of the most universal of musical works, gaining acceptance among all classes and in all lands where European music is appreciated. It has been a standard piece throughout Europe from Haydn's time until our own. In the German-speaking lands especially it has been greatly cherished, and is quite generally regarded as Haydn's masterpiece. The lovable, almost *Biedermeyer* quality of some of Haydn's melodies and tone-painting gave the work a particularly broad appeal in Austria and Germany, while its monumental, Handelian aspect appealed to the more high-minded Romantics. This last characteristic was emphasized by the larger and larger forces that were used in German-language performances in the nineteenth century, especially by the Gesellschaft der Musikfreunde of Vienna (founded 1813).[52] Even when Haydn's symphonies began to lose favour, *The Creation* continued to be adored in Vienna.[53]

The longest and most substantial of the early Austrian reviews,[54] attributed to Carl Friedrich Zelter, singled out the 'Representation of Chaos' for special praise, calling it 'the crown on a royal head', and other

German writers treated this with awe for its genius and harmonic audacity, although a Parisian correspondent produced the unexpected criticism that it did not have *enough* disorder and confusion in it.[55]

Some adverse reactions to the libretto surfaced quite soon in reviews.[56] The one aspect of the work that came under fairly regular attack, especially in German critical writing, was its tone-painting (*Thonmalerei*) or 'naturalism'. This was a device that was rapidly going out of fashion in the developing Romantic aesthetic. It was greeted with rapture in January 1801 by a Berlin correspondent of the *Allgemeine musikalische Zeitung*,[57] but shortly afterwards Friedrich Wilhelm Josef von Schelling wrote scornfully of 'the *illustrative*, something that only a debased and decadent taste can demand of music, taste of the kind that nowadays enjoys the bleating of sheep in Haydn's *Creation*'.[58] Madame de Staël, Arthur Schopenhauer and William Crotch also condemned the tone-painting.[59]

Perhaps the lowest point of *The Creation*'s critical repute came during the high Romantic period. A writer in Schumann's *Neue Zeitschrift für Musik* clearly felt that the work had been overvalued (see p. 96 below). Berlioz, in his ideas about music and especially 'musical imitation', was at the opposite extreme from Haydn. In 1837 he was studiously ambiguous in print: 'Haydn ... in his essentially descriptive works *The Creation* and *The Seasons*, does not seem to have lowered his style appreciably when, in order to follow the poem, he applied imitation to such agreeable noises as the warbling of turtledoves – an imitation that is, moreover, quite exact.'[60] But in a private letter written more than twenty years later he pulled no punches:

The Conservatoire presented Haydn's *Creation* complete last Sunday. I stayed away; I have always felt a profound antipathy for this work . . . . I give you that opinion for what it's worth. Its lowing oxen, its buzzing insects, its light in C which dazzles one like a Carcel lamp, and then its Adam, Uriel, Gabriel, and the flute solos and all the amiabilities really shrivel me up – they make me want to murder somebody. The English love a pudding surrounded with a layer of suet; I detest it. Suet is exactly what surrounds the musical pudding of papa Haydn. Naïveté is all very fine, but too much of it we don't need! ... I wouldn't give an apple for the privilege of meeting Eve in the woods; I am sure she is stupid enough to bring shame to the good God, and is just what her husband deserves. . . .

Don't scold me, don't beat me, don't silence me, I will keep quiet of my own accord. In any case, perhaps I am misjudging you. It is perfectly possible that you are no more crazy about *The Creation* and its animals than I am myself. You see the effect of good health: I utter impieties . . . evidently I'm getting better.[61]

In Austria *The Creation*, together with *The Seasons*, acquired a public stature almost equivalent to that of *Messiah* in England: it was above argument. Ritual performances on a grand scale were offered almost every year by the Tonkünstler-Societät, which was reconstituted as the Haydn-Societät in 1862; the Gesellschaft der Musikfreunde performed *The Creation* eight times between 1876 and 1908.[62] But this constant repetition greatly annoyed Eduard Hanslick, who was not interested in Haydn.[63]

Critical opinion in this period tended to see Beethoven as the founder of modern music and to belittle his predecessors. Theodor Billroth in 1898 asked if 'it is not impossible that in not too far a time in the future, *every* piece of music written before Beethoven will be put aside as not interesting enough'.[64] (As it turned out this could hardly have been a more misguided prophecy of twentieth-century musical taste!) The late Romantics admired Haydn, if at all, for what they perceived as his innocence; Hugo Wolf wrote of *The Creation* in 1885: 'What a spirit of childlike faith speaks from the heavenly pure tones of Haydn's music! Sheer nature, artlessness, perception and sensitivity!'[65] An exception was made for the 'Representation of Chaos', which was treated as an extraordinary precursor of later developments, whose boldness could still surprise. This movement, alone, was later honoured with a detailed analysis by Heinrich Schenker.[66] Along these lines, Paul Dukas in 1904 made an intelligent comparison of Haydn's and Berlioz's approach to musical description (see p. 100 below).

Opinion in England was coloured from the start by two negative factors: first, the feeling that Haydn had set himself up as a rival to Handel, the great national composer; second, the defects of the English text and (even more) the unfortunate way it had been fitted to the music. In some quarters there was disapproval of the text on another ground: that the exchanges between Adam and Eve were too suggestive of sexual activity.[67] William Gardiner, an influential writer and amateur musician, was captivated by the 'Chaos', which he called 'a treasure of sublimity, [in which] we find every voice and instrument conspiring to raise the mind of man to contemplate the wonderful work of God'.[68] But Thomas Busby was scathing, withholding praise even from Haydn's orchestration – indeed, from everything except the 'Light':

... what are the real and prominent features of this composition? A series of attempted imitations of many things inimitable by music, the sudden creation of light happily expressed by an unexpected burst of sound, airs not abundantly beautiful or original, smothered with ingenious accompaniments, and choruses in which the composer toils under his incumbent weight, labours in fugue, copies with faint pencil the clear lustre of a glorious prototype, and supplies the absence of a true taste and dignity, with the congregated powers of a complicated band.[69]

In Victorian times it seems to have been the Nonconformists who chiefly maintained *The Creation*'s reputation. It remained a favourite with the great choral societies of the north of England,[70] and the Sacred Harmonic Society performed it once or twice every year at Exeter Hall, London.[71] Five distinct English editions appeared in the 1840s. In an analytical essay published in 1854, George Alexander Macfarren wrote a sympathetic account of the work, and yet seemed to distance himself from the popular enthusiasm that was then perhaps at its height (see p. 96).

But by 1908 *The Creation* had 'dropped out of the repertories of London and provincial choral societies'.[72] Critical opinions had steadily declined, while Haydn's 'London' symphonies and string quartets remained in favour (the reverse of the situation in Austria). In 1899 an English writer could call *The Creation* 'a third-rate Oratorio, whose interest is largely historic and literary'.[73]

Haydn's reputation improved little in the early decades of the present century, and it is hard to find from this period any serious writing dealing with *The Creation* except as a historical phenomenon.[74] Landon sees the upward reevaluation of Haydn as beginning in the 1930s. In England he was championed by the most influential critic of the time, Donald Tovey; German opinion moved in the same direction after World War II.

Tovey decided that 'the time [was] ripe for a better understanding of Haydn's *Creation* than can be inculcated by fashion'.[75] He praised the work in a brilliant if somewhat patronizing essay written for an Edinburgh performance in 1934 (see p. 103), and since that time there has been a steady rise in its English reputation. Surprisingly, the first complete recording was not made until 1944, and it seems to have been a turning point in the work's reputation outside the German-speaking lands (it had never gone out of popular favour within them). The writings of Karl Geiringer, Jens Peter Larsen and H. C. Robbins Landon have opened our eyes once more to Haydn's greatness. His stature has grown almost to what it was in 1800; from our distance of time he is no longer dwarfed by the proximate bulk of Beethoven, nor do we any longer feel affronted by his apparent challenge to Handel. Few today find any difficulty in accepting the naturalism of Haydn's illustrations. Interestingly enough, Tovey, even as he put this prejudice to rest, instilled new life into another: that the love duet (No. 32) was unworthy of the subject and should be discarded.[76]

Perhaps the most perceptive discussion of *The Creation* in recent times is that of Charles Rosen. His general thesis is that 'the classical style is at its most problematic in religious music', and that Haydn's masses 'remain ... uncomfortable compromises'.[77] He continues:

Haydn's escape was through his beloved pastoral. In neither *The Creation* nor the *Seasons* is the high level of writing always as successfully and as continuously sustained as in the great symphonies and quartets (although the less admired *Seasons* seem to me more successful in this respect), but they are among the greatest works of the century, and music of specifically religious character settles with ease in a framework that allows it to escape from liturgical constraints. Above all, the pastoral tradition provided unequivocal solutions to the problem of setting a text which the late eighteenth-century religious style, corrupted by logical contradictions, was no longer capable of giving. In particular, the pastoral accommodated itself without misgivings to the shape of the 'sonata', which it had, after all, helped to create.[78]

Rosen points out that 'the imposed simplicity of the pastoral style was the condition which made it possible to grasp subjects of such immensity ... The subject of pastoral is not Nature itself, but man's relation to nature and to what is "natural"'.[79]

We have perhaps learned, after two centuries of more and more comprehensive historicism, to seek out the meaning of a work for its composer and his contemporaries, and then to accept or reject it on those terms. The various prejudices, religious and aesthetic, have gradually fallen away. We can now understand *The Creation* as a statement of warm optimism about the world and our place in it, clothed in some of the most gorgeous music of music's golden age. We may well look back with sadness and envy to a time when a composer could say such things, and men and women could hear them, in a spirit of simple confidence.

> Schöne Welt, wo bist du? Kehre wieder,
> holdes Blüthenalter der Natur![80]

5

Design of the work

Overall plan

The Creation is blessed with one of the strongest and most logical large-scale structures in eighteenth-century vocal music. No setting of the Mass can equal it in this respect, because the shape of the Mass Ordinary is intractably lopsided: this often created problems in a period when balance and symmetry were basic aesthetic assumptions. The *St Matthew Passion*, *Saul* and *Messiah* had structures as sturdy as *The Creation*'s; among the masterpieces of the classical period perhaps only *Così fan tutte* is its equal in this respect.

Strength of design was the best feature of the original English libretto, and fortunately it was not fatally weakened by van Swieten's cuts and alterations. So Haydn was able to develop his symphonic and operatic gifts, together with his more recently acquired understanding of Handelian choral writing, within a framework that balanced all these elements and showed them to their best advantage.

The oratorio falls into three parts, the first two roughly equal in length and the third somewhat shorter. Each part is clearly subdivided into groups of movements ending with a triumphant chorus. There are seven such groups in all, as shown in Table 1. Thus, as the angels narrate and comment on the successive wonders of the natural world, and then (in Part Three) Adam and Eve gaze on the new world and find each other's love, each development is crowned by a choral movement that brings together all the available forces and raises to new heights the uplifting effect of the preceding group of movements. The emotional direction is almost constantly upward.

There is, moreover, a cumulative effect that corresponds precisely with the creation story itself. On the First Day, the Representation of Chaos

Table 1. Overall plan of *The Creation*

Movements	Subject matter	Chorus of praise	Key of chorus
Part One			
{ 1–2	First Day: creation of heaven, earth, light		
{ 3	Second Day: division of the waters	4	C
5–9	Third Day: land and sea; plant life	10	D
11–12	Fourth Day: sun, moon, stars	13	C
Part Two			
14–18	Fifth Day: birds and fish; command to multiply	19	A
20–5	Sixth Day: beasts; man and woman	26–8	Bb
Part Three			
29	Adam and Eve's awakening	30	C
31–3	Adam and Eve's mutual love	34	Bb

generates a high tension which is dissipated by the creation of light and the quietly confident chorus (No. 2) welcoming the 'new created world'. After the division of the waters on the Second Day, the vaults resound to a more brilliant chorus. The Third Day witnesses the formation of the earthly landscape, and this time the chorus includes a fully worked-out fugue. The sun, moon and stars follow on the Fourth Day, and are greeted with the climactic C-major chorus 'The heavens are telling', which ends Part One.

In Part Two, the creation of animal life is described in full detail on the Fifth Day, which takes much longer than its predecessors, and the chorus of praise is surmounted by coloratura display from the angel soloists. Finally, by way of climax, man and woman appear on the Sixth Day, the crowning glory of creation. This time the praise takes up three movements (Nos. 26–8): a chorus, a trio of angels, and a return of the chorus, now extended by a double fugue. In Part Three Adam and Eve appear and are joined by the chorus in a great Hymn. The following love duet descends to a less sublime level, thereby enhancing the power of the last chorus, with its great double fugue, unison climax and conclusive Amen.

It is a structure with little dramatic conflict or contrast, and almost no tension after the opening movement. But these are replaced by continuous motion in a single, positive direction: one which Haydn, at the very height of his powers, had the resources to sustain over nearly two hours of music.

Musical unity

A plan of this kind hardly needed musical props, and we find little or no attempt on Haydn's part to 'unify' the oratorio by either thematic or tonal means. Thematic links between movements were rare in eighteenth-century music (except, of course, in genres such as the variation partita, chorale cantata or *cantus firmus* mass). Mozart in his operas tended to choose an overall tonality – at least to the extent that they began and ended in the same key – and, in the later works, to use one or two motto themes. There is no convincing evidence that Haydn followed these precedents.

Some critics have claimed that *The Creation* has an overall tonality of C major: this is the position of Siegmund Levarie, who says that the Bb ending symbolizes man's 'fall from grace'.[1] Now since the work does *not* begin and end in the same key, the only way to establish that the ending in a different key is significant is to show, by other evidence, that a C-major ending would have been expected. This would be the case either if oratorios normally ended in the key in which they began, or if, in this particular work, a specially strong expectation of C major had been built up.

None of the Handel oratorios known to Haydn and the Viennese has an overall tonality. The nearest case is *Samson*. Its overture is in G, but the opening of the First Act and the end of the work are both in D, to take advantage of trumpets. According to Smither, an oratorio in the classical period 'usually begins and ends in the same key',[2] and this is the case with Haydn's *Il ritorno di Tobia*, which has an overture in C minor-major and a final chorus in C major, though no intermediate movement was in that key in the original score.[3] But *The Seven Last Words* begins in D minor and ends in C minor, with 'no discernible pattern of key organization'.[4] In *The Seasons* the fourth part, 'Winter', begins in C minor and ends in C major, but the other three parts – and the whole – begin and end in different keys.

These facts show that there is, *prima facie*, no very strong reason to suppose that contemporary audiences would have expected *The Creation* to end in C major. Nor is the internal evidence compelling. Of course, many keys can be 'related' to C major in some way, but to form an expectation in the listener, or even the score-reader, it would be necessary to have either a preponderant emphasis on C in earlier movements or a clear tonal progression that appeared to be moving towards C at the end. Neither exists here. In Parts One and Two the only movements in C are Nos. 1 (C minor-major), 4, 13 and 24. True, these are significant movements;[5] but the memory of their key is obliterated by the tremendously strong assertion of Bb major at the end of Part Two, where the whole of creation is celebrated in the choruses Nos. 26 and 28, with an Eb trio between them, but with no implication, surely, of the coming Fall.

In this context, Part Three opens in the extremely remote key of E major (Tovey wanted to omit the customary interval between Parts in order to 'give its proper Beethovenish effect to Haydn's extreme contrast between B flat and E major'[6]). A cycle of descending fifths leads to a stable C major for the Hymn (No. 30), with its long middle section in F. But, after a widely modulating recitative, the two closing movements are in Eb and Bb. For the rare listener with absolute pitch or longterm tonal memory, these must surely suggest a return to the keys that ended Part Two rather than a deviation from an expected continuation in C. It seems that a C-major 'plan' is perceived only by an observer who deliberately shuts out all countervailing evidence.

Landon, while accepting Levarie's conclusion that 'the basic key of *The Creation* is C,'[7] also states that '*The Creation* is in progressive tonality' (he says the same about *The Seasons*).[8] However, he offers no definition of this concept, merely providing a diagram with arrows connecting the keys of all the movements. Nobody has established that the succession of keys points compellingly towards C major or, indeed, any other tonality.

We may be sure that Haydn was concerned with the progression of keys from one movement to the next within each Part; unlike supposed overall key schemes, these relationships are readily perceived by every musical listener. It is also probable that he was influenced by the conventional understanding of the characteristics of keys, as described by Christian Friedrich Daniel Schubart (1739–91) and many other contemporary theorists. Although Haydn himself is not known to have expressed views on this subject, movements from *The Creation* were cited by several early-nineteenth-century writers to exemplify key characteristics.[9] Above all, the movement from C minor to C major depicting the change from darkness to light, from chaos to cosmos, is heavy with symbolism – whether Christian, Deist, Masonic or none of these – that could be taken to celebrate the Enlightenment itself.

The first two movements, indeed, remarkably extend this symbolic key relationship. Chaos is in C minor, with Eb major as complementary key (and with still further excursions on the flat side: to Eb minor, in bars 16–19 and 32–5, and Db major, in 21–5). Raphael returns to Eb, with another foray into Eb minor, when speaking of darkness. Light blazes forth in C major. No. 2 follows with a corresponding movement on the sharp side, to A major. Light has replaced darkness, order disorder; but twice in the course of this movement 'hell's spirits black in throngs' reappear. The tonality plunges all the way back to C minor the first time and is gradually brought back to A minor, then A major. On the second occasion (bars 113–25), the powers of hell are evidently enfeebled, and only manage to drag the tonality down as far as A minor. Then they disappear for good and A major triumphs. Haydn's management of these remote modulations seems quite effortless, and it anticipates by about a generation the much-vaunted Romantic use of 'third relationships' among keys.[10]

But if C minor to C major indicates the coming of light and the defeat of the forces of darkness, that idea is not the only one emphasized in this account of creation. The appearance of man, to lord it over nature and uniquely to praise his maker, is the obvious climax of the story, and if any one key expresses this idea in Haydn's conception it is the key of Bb.

Text and musical treatment

In the libretto that follows, the German and English texts are those of the first edition; original spellings, punctuation, and capitalization have been retained, but accidental errors have been silently corrected. Movement numbers follow the standard numbering in the Eulenburg and Peters editions. German movement headings are from the first edition, English headings are translations of these. Movement headings in brackets are from other authentic sources. Italic titles of groups of movements within each part are editorial. After the texts of each movement, a brief musical description has been provided; the terms used are discussed in chapter 6. Both here and in chapter 6 keys are given in upper or lower case to indicate major or minor mode.

DIE SCHÖPFUNG

THE CREATION

Characters: Gabriel (soprano), Eve (soprano), Uriel (tenor), Raphael (bass), Adam (bass)

Chorus (SATB) with soloists (SATB)

Orchestration: 3 flutes, 2 oboes, 2 clarinets, 2 bassoons, contrabassoon, 2 horns, 2 trumpets, 3 trombones, timpani, strings, and keyboard continuo

ERSTER THEIL

PART ONE

The First Day

1. Einleitung: Die Vorstellung des Chaos

1. Introduction: The Representation of Chaos

(Orchestral introduction; c, Largo, ¢, 59 bars)

Recitativo (Raphael)

Recitative (Raphael)

Im Anfange schuf Gott Himmel und Erde; und die Erde war ohne Form und leer; und Finsterniss war auf der Fläche der Tiefe.

In the beginning God created the Heave and the earth; and the earth was without for and void; and darkness was upon the face the deep.

(Accompanied recitative, c – Eb, 16 bars)

Coro

Und der Geist Gottes schwebte auf der Fläche der Wasser; und Gott sprach: Es werde Licht, und es ward Licht.

Chorus

And the Spirit of God moved upon the face of the waters; and God said: Let there be Light, and there was Light.

(Largely homophonic; Eb – c – C, [Largo], ¢, 14 bars)

Recitativo (Uriel)

Und Gott sah das Licht, das es gut war: und Gott schied das Licht von der Finsterniss.

Recitative (Uriel)

And God saw the Light, that it was good: and God divided the Light from the darkness.

(Accompanied recitative, C, 7 bars)

2. Aria (Uriel)

Nun schwanden vor dem heiligen Strahle
des schwarzen Dunkels gräuliche Schatten;
der erste Tag enstand.
Verwirrung weicht, und Ordnung keimt
empor.
Erstarrt entflieht der Höllengeister Schaar

in des Abgrunds Tiefen hinab,
zur ewigen Nacht.

Chor. Verzweiflung, Wuth und Schrecken
begleiten ihren Sturz.
Und ein neüe Welt
entspringt auf Gottes Wort.

2. Air [with Chorus] (Uriel)

Now vanish before the holy beams
the gloomy dismal shades of dark;
the first of days appears.
Disorder yields to order fair the place.

Affrighted fled hell's spirits black in
throngs;
down they sink in the deep of abyss
to endless night.

Despairing cursing rage
attends their rapid fall.
A new created world
springs up at God's command.

(Sectional form: A – E, Andante, ¢; c – A, Allegro moderato, C, 150 bars)

The Second Day

3. Recitativo (Raphael)

Und Gott machte das Firmament, und theilte die Wasser, die unter dem Firmament waren, von den Gewässern, die ober dem Firmament waren, und es ward so.

3. Recitative (Raphael)

And God made the firmament, and divided the waters, which were under the firmament, from the waters, which were above the firmament, and it was so.

(Secco recitative, 6 bars)

[mit Begleitung]

Da tobten brausend heftige Stürme;
Wie Spreü vor dem Winde, so flogen die
Wolken.
Die Luft durchschnitten feurige Blitze,
und schrecklich rollten die Donner umher.

[Accompanied]

Outrageous storms now dreadful arose;
as chaff by the winds are impellèd the
clouds.
By heaven's fire the sky is enflamed
and awfull rolled the thunders on high.

Der Fluth enstieg auf sein Geheiss der allerquickende Regen, der allverheerende Schauer, der leichte flockige Schnee.	Now from the floods in steams ascend reviving showers of rain, the dreary wasteful hail, the light and flaky snow.

(Accompanied recitative; F – C, Allegro assai, **C**, 37 bars; linked to …)

4. Chor

4. Chorus [with solo: Gabriel]

G	Mit Staunen sieht das Wunderwerk der Himmelsbürger frohe Schaar	The marv'lous work beholds amaz'd the glorious hierarchy of Heav'n
G,Chor.	und laut ertönt aus ihren Kehlen des Schöpfers Lob, das Lob des zweyten Tags.	and to th' ethereal vaults resound the praise of God. and of the second day.

(Binary form; C, Allegro, **C**, 49 bars)

The Third Day

5. Recitativo (Raphael)

5. Recitative (Raphael)

Und Gott sprach: Es sammle sich das Wasser unter dem Himmel zusammen an einem Platz, und es erscheine das trockne Land; und es ward so.

Und Gott nannte das trockne Land: Erde, und die Sammlung der Wasser nannte er Meer; und Gott sah, dass es gut war.

And God said: Let the waters under the heaven be gathered together unto one place, and let the dry land appear; and it was so.

And God called the dry land: earth, and the gathering of waters called he seas; and God saw that it was good.

(Secco recitative, 12 bars)

6. Aria (Raphael)

6. Air (Raphael)

Rollend in schäumenden Wellen
bewegt sich ungestüm das Meer.
Hügel und Felsen erscheinen;
der Berge Gipfel steigt empor.
Die Fläche, weit gedehnt, durchläuft
der breite Strohm in mancher Krümme.
Leise rauschend gleitet fort
im stillen Thal der helle Bach.

Rolling in foaming billows
uplifted roars the boist'rous sea.
Mountains and rocks now emerge;
their tops into the clouds ascend.
Thro' th'open plains outstretching wide
in serpent error rivers flow.
Softly purling glides on
thro' silent vales the limpid brook.

(Sectional form; d – D, Allegro assai, **C**, 121 bars)

7. Recitativo (Gabriel)

7. Recitative (Gabriel)

Und Gott sprach: Es bringe die Erde Gras hervor, Kräuter, die Samen geben, und Obstbäume, die Früchte bringen ihrer Art gemäss, die ihren Samen in sich selbst haben auf der Erde; und es ward so.

And God said: Let the earth bring forth grass, the herb yielding seed, and the fruit tree yielding fruit after his kind, whose seed is in itself upon the earth; and it was so.

(Secco recitative, 9 bars)

8. Aria (Gabriel)	8. Air (Gabriel)
Nun beut die Flur das frische Grün dem Auge zur Ergetzung dar;	With verdure clad the fields appear delightful to the ravish'd sense;
den anmuthsvollen Blick erhöh't der Blumen sanfter Schmuck.	by flowers sweet and gay enhanced is the charming sight.
Hier düften Kräuter Balsam aus; hier sprosst den Wunden Heil.	Here vent their fumes the fragrant herbs, here shoots the healing plant.
Die Zweige krümmt der goldnen Früchte Last;	By loads of fruit th'expanded boughs are press'd;
hier wölbt der Hain zum kühlen Schirme sich; den steilen Berg bekrönt ein dichter Wald.	to shady vaults are bent the tufty groves; the mountain's brow is crown'd with closed wood.

(Transformed da capo form; B♭, Andante, 6/8, 89 bars)

9. Recitativo (Uriel)	9. Recitative (Uriel)
Und die himmlischen Heerschaaren verkündigten den dritten Tag, Gott preisend und sprechend:	And the heavenly host proclaimed the third day, praising God and saying:

(Secco recitative, 4 bars; linked to ...)

10. Chor	10. Chorus
Stimmt an die Saiten, ergreift die Leyer!	Awake the harp, the lyre awake!
Lasst euer Lobgesang erschallen!	In shout and joy your voices raise!
Frohlocket dem Herrn, dem mächtigen Gott!	In triumph sing the mighty Lord!
Denn er hat Himmel und Erde bekleidet in herrlicher Pracht.	For he the heavens and earth has cloathèd in stately dress.

(Chorus with fugue; D, Vivace, **c**, 56 bars)

The Fourth Day

11. Recitativo (Uriel)	11. Recitative (Uriel)
Und Gott sprach: Es seyn Lichter an der Feste des Himmels, um den Tag von der Nacht zu scheiden, und Licht auf der Erde zu geben; und es seyn diese für Zeichen und für Zeiten, und für Tage, und für Jahre. Er machte die Sterne gleichfalls.	And God said: Let there be lights in the firmament of heaven to divide the day from the night, and to give light upon the earth; and let them be for signs and for seasons, and for days, and for years. He made the stars also.

(Secco recitative, 11 bars)

55

12. Recitativo (Uriel)

In vollem Glanze steiget jezt
  die Sonne strahlend auf;
ein wonnevoller Bräutigam,
  ein Riese stolz und froh
  zu rennen seine Bahn.
(a tempo)
Mit leisen Gang und sanften Schimmer
  schleicht
der Mond die stille Nacht hindurch.

(ad libitum)
  Den ausgedehnten Himmelsraum
ziert ohne Zahl der hellen Sterne Gold,
und die Söhne Gottes verkündigten den
vierten Tag mit Himmlischen Gesang, seine
Macht ausrufend also:

12. Recitative (Uriel)

In splendor bright is rising now
  the sun and darts his rays;
an am'rous joyful happy spouse,
  a giant proud and glad
  to run his measur'd course.

With softer beams and milder light steps on

  the silver moon through silent night.

  The space immense of th'azure sky
innum'rous host of radiant orbs adorns,
and the sons of God announced the fourth
day in song divine, proclaiming thus his power:

(Accompanied recitative; D – G – C, 50 bars; linked to . . .)

13. Chor

Die Himmel erzählen die Ehre Gottes.
Und seiner Hände Werk zeigt an das
  Firmament.

Gabriel, Uriel, Raphael

Dem kommenden Tage sagt es der Tag;
die Nacht, die verschwand, der folgenden
  Nacht.

Tutti

Die Himmel erzählen . . .

Gabriel, Uriel, Raphael

In alle Welt ergeht das Wort,
jedem Ohre klingend, keiner Zunge
  fremd.

Tutti

Die Himmel erzählen . . .

13. Chorus [with Trio]

The heavens are telling the glory of God.
The wonder of his works displays the
  firmament.

To day, that is coming, speaks it the day;
the night, that is gone, to following night.

The heavens are telling . . .

In all the land resounds the word,
never unperceivèd, ever understood.

The heavens are telling . . .

(Chorus with fugato; C, Allegro – Più allegro, ¢, 196 bars)

ZWEITER THEIL	**PART TWO**

The Fifth Day

14. Recitativo (Gabriel)	14. Recitative (Gabriel)

Und Gott sprach: Es bringe das Wasser in der Fülle hervor webende Geschöpfe, die Leben haben, und Vögel, die über der Erde fliegen mögen in dem offenen Firmamente des Himmels.	And God said: Let the waters bring forth abundantly the moving creature that hath life, and fowl, that may fly above the earth in the open firmament of heaven.

(Accompanied recitative; C – F, Allegro, 11 bars)

15. Aria (Gabriel)	15. Aria (Gabriel)

Auf starkem Fittige schwinget sich der Adler stolz, und theilet die Luft im schnellesten Fluge zur Sonne hin. Den Morgen grüsst der Lerche frohes Lied, und Liebe girrt das zarte Tauben paar. Aus jedem Busch und Hain erschallt der Nachtigallen süsse Kehle. Noch drückte Gram nicht ihre Brust, noch war zur Klage nicht gestimmt ihr reitzender Gesang.	On mighty pens uplifted soars the eagle aloft, and cleaves the sky in swiftest flight to the blazing sun. His welcome bids to morn the merry lark, and cooing, calls the tender dove his mate. From ev'ry bush and grove resound the nightingale's delightful notes. No grief affected yet her breast, nor to a mournful tale were tun'd her soft enchanting lays.

(Free binary form; F. Moderato, ¢, 207 bars)

16. Recitativo (Raphael)	16. Recitative (Raphael)

Und Gott schuf grosse Wallfische, und ein jedes lebende Geschöpf, das sich beweget. Und Gott segnete sie, sprechend:	And God created great whales, and ev'ry living creature that moveth. And God blessed them, saying:

(Secco recitative, 5 bars)

In tempo	[Recitative] In tempo

Seyd fruchtbar alle, mehret euch! Bewohner der Luft, vermehret euch, und singt auf jedem Aste! Mehret euch, ihr Fluthenbewohner, und füllet jede Tiefe! Seyd fruchtbar, wachset, mehret euch! Erfreuet euch in eurem Gott!	Be fruitful all, and multiply! Ye wingèd tribes, be multiply'd, and sing on ev'ry tree! Multiply, ye finny tribes, and fill each wat'ry deep! Be fruitful, grow, and multiply! And in your God and Lord rejoice!

(Accompanied recitative; d, Poco adagio, ¢, 17 bars)

17. Ad libitum (Raphael)	17. Recitative (Raphael)

Und die Engel rührten ihr unsterblichen Harpfen, und sangen die Wunder des fünften Tags.	And the angels struck their immortal harps, and the wonders of the fifth day sung.

(Secco recitative, 6 bars)

18. Terzetto (Gabriel, Uriel, Raphael)

G In holder Anmuth steh'n,
mit jungem Grün geschmückt,
die wogichten Hügel da.
Aus ihren Adern quillt,
in fliessendem Kristall,
der kühlende Bach hervor.

U In frohen Kreisen schwebt,
sich wiegend in der Luft,
der munteren Vögel Schaar.
Den bunten Federglanz
erhöh't im Wechselflug,
das goldene Sonnenlicht.

R Das helle Nass durchblitzt
der Fisch, und windet sich
in stätem Gewühl' umher.
Vom tiefsten Meeresgrund
wälzt sich Leviathan
auf schäumender Well'empor.

G,U,R Wie viel sind deiner Werk, O Gott!
Wer fasset ihre Zahl?
Wer, O Gott?
Wer fasset ihre Zahl?

18. Trio (Gabriel, Uriel, Raphael)

Most beautyfull appear,
with verdure young adorn'd,
the gently sloping hills.
Their narrow, sinuous veins
distill in crystal drops
the fountain fresh and bright.

In lofty circles plays
and hovers thro' the sky
the chearful host of birds.
And in the flying whirl,
the glitt'ring plumes are died,
as rainbows, by the sun.

See flashing thro' the wet
in throngèd swarms the fry
on thousand ways around.
Upheaved from the deep,
th'immense Leviathan
sports on the foaming wave.

How many are thy works, O God!
Who may their numbers tell?
Who, O God?
Who may their numbers tell?

(Varied srophic song with coda; A, Moderato, 2/4; linked to . . .)

19. Chor

Der Herr ist gross in seiner Macht,
und ewig bleibt sein Ruhm.

19. Chorus [with Trio]

The Lord is great, and great his might.
His glory lasts
for ever and for evermore.

(A, Vivace, **c**, 65 bars)

The Sixth Day

20. Recitativo (Raphael)

Und Gott sprach: Es bringe die Erde hervor
lebende Geschöpfe nach ihrer Art; Vieh und
kriechendes Gewürm, und Thiere der Erde
nach ihren Gattungen.

20. Recitative (Raphael)

And God said: Let the earth bring forth the
living creature after his kind; cattle and creep-
ing thing, and beasts of the earth after their
kind.

58

(Secco recitative, 7 bars)

21. Recitativo (Raphael)	21. Recitative (Raphael)

Gleich öffnet sich der Erde Schoss,
und sie gebiert auf Gottes Wort
    Geschöpfe jeder Art,
in vollem Wuchs und ohne Zahl.
Vor Freüde brüllend steht der Löwe da.
Hier schiesst der gelenkige Tyger empor.
Das zackig Haupt erhebt der schnelle
    Hirsch.
    Mit fliegender Mähne springt und
    wieh'rt,
    voll Muth und Kraft, das edle Ross.
    Auf grünen Matten weidet schon
    das Rind, in Heerden abgetheilt.
    Die Triften deckt, als wie gesät,

    das wollenreiche sanfte Schaf.
    Wie Staub verbreitet sich
in Schwarm und Wirbel das Heer der
    Insekte.
    In langen Zügen kriecht
    am Boden das Gewürm.

Strait opening her fertile womb,
    the earth obey'd the word, and teem'd
    creatures numberless,
    in perfect forms and fully grown.
Cheerful, roaring, stands the tawny lion.
In sudden leaps the flexible tiger appears.
The nimble stag bears up his branching
    head.
With flying mane and fiery look,

impatient neighs the sprightly steed.
The cattle in herds already seeks
    his food on fields and meadows green.
And o'er the ground, as plants, are
    spread
    the fleecy, meek and bleating flock.
    Unnumber'd as the sands
in whirl arose the host of insects.

In long dimensions creeps
    with sinuous trace the worm.

(Accompanied recitative; Bb – Db – A – D, Presto – Andante – Adagio, 64 bars)

22. Aria (Raphael)	22. Air (Raphael)

Nun scheint in vollem Glanze der Himmel;
nun prangt in ihrem Schmucke die Erde.

Die Luft erfüllt das leichte Gefieder;
die Wässer schwellt der Fische
    Gewimmel;
den Boden drückt der Thiere Last.

Doch war noch alles nicht vollbracht.
Dem Ganzen fehlte das Geschöpf,
das Gottes Werke dankbar seh'n,
des Herren Güte preisen soll.

Now heav'n in fullest glory shone;
earth smiles in all her rich attire.

The room of air with fowl is fill'd;
the water swell'd by shoals of fish;

by heavy beasts the ground is trod.

But all the work was not complete.
There wanted yet that wondrous being,
that grateful should God's pow'r admire,
with heart and voice his goodness praise.

(Free binary form; D, Maestoso, 3/4, 109 bars)

23. Recitativo (Uriel)	23. Recitative (Uriel)

Und Gott schuf den Menschen nach seinem
Ebenbilde. Nach dem Ebenbilde Gottes schuf

And God created man in his own image. In
the image of God created he him. Male and

59

er ihn. Mann und Weib erschuf er sie. Den Athem des Lebens hauchte er in sein Angesicht, und der Mensch wurde zur lebendigen Seele.

female created he him. He breathed into his nostrils the the breath of life, and man became a living soul.

(Secco recitative, 11 bars)

24. Aria (Uriel)

Mit Würd' und Hoheit angethan,
mit Schönheit, Stärk', und Muth begabt,
gen Himmel aufgerichtet, steht
    der Mensch,
ein Mann, und König der Natur.

Die breit gewölbt erhab'ne Stirn
verkünd't der Weisheit tiefen Sinn,
und aus dem hellen Blicke strahlt
    der Geist,
des Schöpfers Hauch und Ebenbild.

An seinen Busen schmieget sich,
für ihn, aus ihm geformt,
die Gattinn hold, und anmuthsvoll.

In froher Unschuld lächelt sie,
des Frühlings reitzend Bild,
ihm Liebe, Glück und Wonne zu.

24. Air (Uriel)

In native worth and honour clad,
with beauty, courage, strength adorn'd,
to heav'n erect and tall, he stands
    a man,
the Lord and King of nature all.

The large and archèd front sublime
of wisdom deep declares the seat,
and in his eyes with brightness shines
    the soul,
the breath and image of his God.

With fondness leans upon his breast
the partner for him form'd,
a woman fair and graceful spouse.

Her softly smiling virgin looks,
of flow'ry spring the mirror,
bespeak him love, and joy, and bliss.

(Free binary form; C, Andante, **c**, 103 bars)

25. Recitativo (Raphael)

  Und Gott sah jedes Ding, was er gemacht hatte; und es war sehr gut; und der himmlische Chor feyerte das Ende des sechsten Tages mit lautem Gesang.

25. Recitative (Raphael)

  And God saw ev'ry thing, that he had made; and behold, it was very good; and the heavenly choir in song divine thus closed the sixth day.

(Secco recitative, 8 bars)

26. Chor

Vollendet ist das grosse Werk;
der Schöpfer sieht's und freuet sich.
Auch unsre Freud', erschalle laut;
Des Herren Lob sey unser Lied.

26. Chorus

Atchieved is the glorious work;
the Lord beholds it and is pleas'd.
In lofty strains let us rejoice!
Our song let be the praise of God.

(Chorus with fugato; Bb, Vivace, **c**, 37 bars)

27. [Terzetto]

G,U   Zu dir, o Herr, blickt alles auf;
       um Speise fleht dich alles an.

27. [Trio]

On thee each living soul awaits;
from thee, O Lord, they beg their meat.

	Du öffnest dein Hand,	Thou openest thy hand,
	gesättigt werden sie.	and sated all they are.
R	Du wendest ab dein Angesicht;	But as to them thy face is hid,
	da bebet alles und erstarrt.	with sudden terror they are struck.
	Du nimmst dein Odem weg;	Thou tak'st their breath away;
	in Staub zerfallen sie.	they vanish into dust.
G,U,R	Den Odem hauchst du wieder aus,	Thou lett'st thy breath go forth again,
	und neues Leben sprosst hervor.	and life with vigour fresh returns.
	Verjüngt ist die Gestalt	Revived earth unfolds
	der Erd' an Reitz und Kraft.	new force and new delights.

(Transformed da capo form; Eb, Poco adagio, 3/4, 94 bars; linked to . . .)

28. [Coro]   28. [Chorus]

Vollendet ist das grosse Werk.   [Atchieved is the glorious work.
Des Herren Lob sey unser Lied.   Our song let be the praise of God.]
Alles lobe seinen Nahmen;   Glory to his name for ever;
denn er allein ist hoch erhaben,   he sole on high exalted reigns,
alleluja.   [alleluia].

(Chorus with fugue; Bb, Vivace, ¢, 76 bars)

DRITTER THEIL   ## PART THREE

Adam and Eve in Eden

29. Recitativo (Uriel)   29. Recitative (Uriel)

(Orchestral introduction; E, Largo, 3/4, 24 bars)

Aus Rosen wolken bricht,   In rosy mantle appears,
geweckt durch süssen Klang,   by tunes sweet awak'd,
der Morgen jung und schön.   the morning young and fair.
Vom himmlischen Gewölbe   From the celestial vaults
ströhmt reine Harmonie   pure harmony descends
   zur Erde hinab.   on ravishèd earth.
Seht das beglückte Paar,   Behold the blissful pair,
wie Hand in Hand es geht!   where hand in hand they go!
Aus ihren Blicken strahlt   Their flaming looks express
des heissen Danks Gefühl.   what feels the grateful heart.
Bald singt in lautem Ton   A louder praise of God
ihr Mund des Schöpfers Lob.   their lips shall utter soon.
Lasst unsre Stimme dann   Then let our voices ring,
sich mengen in ihr Lied!   united with their song!

(Accompanied recitative; E – G, Largo – Più moto, 3/4, 36 bars)

61

30. [Lobgesang] (Eva, Adam, chorus)

E,A   Von deiner Güt', o Herr und Gott,
      ist Erd' und Himmel voll.
      Die Welt, so gross, so wunderbar,
      ist deiner Hände Werk.

Chor. Gesegnet sey des Herren Macht!
      Sein Lob erschall' in Ewigkeit!

A   Der Sterne hellster, o wie schön
      verkündest du den Tag!
      Wie schmückst du ihn, o Sonne, du,
      des Weltalls Seel' und Aug'!

Chor. Macht kund auf eurer weiten Bahn
      des Herren Macht und seinen Ruhm!

E   Und du, der Nächte Zierd' und Trost,
      und all das strahlend Heer,
      verbreitet überall sein Lob,
      in eurem Chorgesang!

A   Ihr Elemente, deren Kraft
      stäts neue Formen zeigt,
      ihr Dünst' und Nebel, die der Wind
      versammelt und vertreibt:

E,A,
Chor. Lobsinget alle Gott dem Herrn!
      Gross, wie sein Nahm', ist seine
      Macht.

E   Sanft rauschend lobt, o Quellen, ihn!
      Den Wipfel neigt, ihr Bäum'!
      Ihr Pflanzen düftet, Blumen haucht
      ihm euren Wohlgeruch!

A   Ihr, deren Pfad die Höh'n erklimmt,
      und ihr, die niedrig kriecht,
      ihr, deren Flug die Luft durch-
        schneid't,
      und ihr, im tiefen Nass,

E,A,
Chor. Ihr Thiere. preiset alle Gott!
      Ihn Lobe, was nur Odem hat!

E,A, Ihr dunk'len Hain', ihr Berg' und
      Thal,
      ihr Zeugen uns'res Danks;

---

30. [Hymn] (Eve, Adam, chorus)

By thee with bliss, o bounteous Lord,
      the heav'n and earth are stor'd,
      This world, so great, so wonderful,
      thy mighty hand has fram'd.

For ever blessed be his pow'r!
      His name be ever magnify'd!

Of stars the fairest, o how sweet
      thy smile at dawning morn!
      How brighten'st thou, O sun, the day,
      thou eye and soul of all!

Proclaim in your extended course
      th'almighty pow'r and praise of God!

And thou, that rules the silent night,
      and all ye starry host,
      spread wide and ev'ry where his praise
      in choral songs about!

Ye strong and cumb'rous elements,
      who ceaseless changes make,
      ye dusky mists and dewy steams,
      who rise and fall thro' th' air:

Resound the praise of God our Lord!
      Great is his name, and great his might.

Ye purling fountains, tune his praise,
      and wave your tops, ye pines!
      Ye plants, exhale, ye flowers breathe
      at him your balmy scent!

Ye, that on mountains stately tread,
      and ye, that lowly creep, ˙
      ye birds that sing at heaven's gate,

      and ye, that swim the stream,

Ye living souls, extol the Lord!
      Him celebrate, him magnify!

Ye vallies, hills, and shady woods,

      our raptur'd notes ye heard;

ertönen sollt ihr früh und spät von uns'rem Lobgesang!	from morn to ev'n you shall repeat our grateful hymns of praise.

Chor. Heil dir, o Gott! o Schöpfer, Heil!
      Aus deinem Wort' entstand die Welt,

Hail, bounteous Lord! Almighty, hail!
Thy word call'd forth this wond'rous frame.

      dich bethen Erd' und Himmel an;
      wir preisen dich in Ewigkeit.

Thy pow'r adore the heav'n and earth:
we praise thee now and evermore.

(Part 1: binary form, C, Adagio, **c**, 46 bars; Part 2: free rondo with choral
coda, F – C, Allegretto, 2/4, 340 bars)

31. Recitativo (Eva,Adam)	31. Recitative (Eve,Adam)

A   Nun ist die erste Pflicht erfüllt;
     dem Schöpfer haben wir gedankt.
     Nun folge mir, Gefährtinn meines Lebens!
     Ich leite dich, und jeder Schritt
     weckt neue Freud' in uns'rer Brust,
     zeigt Wunder überall.
     Erkennen sollst du dann,
     welch unaussprechlich Glück
     der Herr uns zugedacht,
     ihn preisen immerdar,
     ihm weihen Herz und Sinn.
     Komm, folge mir! Ich leite dich.
	Our duty we perform'd now,
	in off'ring up to God our thanks.
	Now follow me, dear partner of my life!
	
	Thy guide I'll be, and ev'ry step
	pours new delights into our breast,
	shews wonders ev'ry where.
	Then may'st thou feel and know
	the high degree of bliss
	the Lord allotted us,
	and with devoted heart
	his bounty celebrate.
	Come, follow me! Thy guide I'll be.

E   O du, für den ich ward!
     Mein Schirm, mein Schild, mein All!
     Dein Will' ist mir Gesetz.
     So hat's der Herr bestimmt,
     Und dir gehorchen bringt
     mir Freude, Glück und Ruhm.
	O thou, for whom I am!
	My help, my shield, my all!
	Thy will is law to me.
	So God, our Lord, ordains,
	and from obedience grows
	my pride and happiness.

(Secco recitative, 39 bars)

32. Duetto (Eva,Adam)	32. Duet (Eve,Adam)

A   Holde Gattin! Dir zur Seite
     fliessen sanft die Stunden hin.
     Jeder Augenblick ist Wonne,
     keine Sorge trübet sie.
	Graceful consort! At thy side
	softly fly the golden hours.
	Ev'ry moment brings new rapture,
	ev'ry care is put to rest.

E   Theurer Gatte! Dir zur Seite
     schwimmt in Freuden mir das Herz.
     Dir gewidmet ist mein Leben;
     deine Liebe sey mein Lohn.
	Spouse adored! At thy side
	purest joys o'erflow the heart.
	Life and all I am is thine;
	my reward thy love shall be.

A Der thauende Morgen, o wie ermuntert er!	The dew-dropping morn, O how she quickens all!

E	Die Kühle des Abends, o wie erquicket sie!	The coolness of ev'n, O how she all restores!
A	Wie labend ist der runden Früchte Saft!	How grateful is of fruits the savour sweet!
E	Wie reitzend ist der Blumen süsse Duft!	How pleasing is of fragrant bloom the smell!

E,A Doch ohne dich, was wäre mir

    { der Morgenthau,
    { der Abendhauch,

    { der Früchte Saft,
    { der Blumen Duft?

Mit dir erhöht sich jede Freude,
mit dir geniess' ich doppelt sie;
mit dir ist Seligkeit das Leben;
dir sey es ganz geweiht.

But without thee, what is to me

    { the morning dew,
    { the breath of ev'n,

    { the sav'ry fruit,
    { the fragrant bloom?

With thee is ev'ry joy enhancèd,
with thee delight is ever new;
with thee is life incessant bliss;
thine it whole shall be.

(Modified *rondò*. Part 1: free binary form, E♭, Adagio, 3/4, 71 bars; Part 2: free strophic form, E♭, Allegro, 2/4, 219 bars)

33. Recitativo (Uriel)

O glücklich Paar, und glücklich immerfort,
   wenn falscher Wahn euch nicht
     verführt
noch mehr zu wünschen, als ihr habt,
und mehr zu wissen, als ihr sollt!

33. Recitative (Uriel)

O happy pair, and always happy yet,
   if not, misled by false conceit,

   ye strive at more, as granted is,
   and more to know, as know ye should!

(Secco recitative, 7 bars)

34. Chor

   Singt dem Herren alle Stimmen!
   Dankt ihm alle seine Werke!
   Lasst zu Ehren seines Nahmens
   Lob in Wettgesang erschallen!
Des Herren Ruhm, er bleibt in
   Ewigkeit.
               Amen.

34. Chorus [with soloists]

   Sing the Lord, ye voices all!
   Utter thanks ye all his works!
   Celebrate his pow'r and glory!
   Let his name resound on high!
The Lord is great, his praise shall last for
   aye.
               [Amen.]

(Introduction and fugue; B♭, Andante, **C**, 83 bars)

6

Musical analysis

The following discussion is organized by type of movement. Within each category is incorporated a more detailed description of one or more movements; these are listed in bold type under each heading and in the text.[1]

Secco Recitative

Nos. 3 (bars 1–6), 5, 7, 9, 11, 16 (bars 1–5), 17, 23, 25, **31**, 33

Recitative with *basso continuo* accompaniment only had been invented shortly before 1600 as the most sensitive and expressive kind of music imaginable; and in some seventeenth-century operas and oratorios the recitative soliloquy was reserved for the emotional climax of a work. In modern times simple recitative has been called *secco* (dry). By the end of the eighteenth century, although simple recitative was still an excellent vehicle for spontaneous expression on the part of the singer, composers tended to treat it as a perfunctory part of their craft – perhaps to be dashed off during the last few hours before a performance, or even left to a deputy. The conventions had become almost absolute; the chief skill required of the composer was to steer the tonality towards the next movement.

Haydn perhaps took more care in this case, knowing especially that he was dealing for the most part with biblical words. Italian recitative, with its standard verse form and feminine endings, could not provide examples of the variable rhythm needed for prose, and Haydn had to invent non-conventional cadences and phrases:[2] this can be seen most clearly in No. 5. Almost the only available models for English or German prose recitative were Handel's *Messiah* and *Israel in Egypt*, since Bach's Passions were unknown and unavailable.

The most operatic of the secco recitatives is **No. 31**, at 39 bars by far the longest in the oratorio, and the only one describing human action. It falls between the two largest concerted movements, and for this reason, perhaps, Haydn followed Swieten's suggestion to use secco recitative. The first three bars are much like the earlier examples. Then comes a double bar and a tempo direction, *Allegro*; the mood changes at once to something more operatic. Adam and Eve have done their duty by praising God in the great hymn; now they can turn to the delights of love. The *basso continuo* comes to life for the first time, with a short figure that alludes to No. 26, 'Achieved is the glorious work', again signalling that the time for enjoyment has come. Adam enthusiastically offers to guide his partner in exploring the unknown joys in store for them; the phrase most nearly suggesting stage action in the whole work, 'Come, follow me,' is set in suitably operatic style with short accompaniment chords. After an interrupted cadence on the chord of Gb, Eve answers more demurely ('Thy will is law to me'). With a new tempo mark of *Andante* and a sombre bass figure, she emphasizes that it is God's command, rather than her own wish, that leads her to seek the joys of sex. But Haydn singles out the word *Freude* (closer to 'joy' than to the English text 'pride') for a pause and short coloratura passage (see Ex. 5). Haydn was clearly unembarrassed by the idea that Adam and Eve were about to 'celebrate' physical love – a notion that some English revisers of the text were anxious to suppress.

Example 5 No. 31 (Recitative), bars 35–9

Accompanied recitative

No. 1 (bars 59–75, 89–96), 3 (bars 7–43), 12, 14, **16** (bars 6–22), **21**, 29 (bars 24–60)

I use this term in preference to a number of alternatives to describe recitative with orchestral accompaniment. The style was developed in Metastasian *opera seria* and oratorio, where it was normally reserved for a spritual crisis, to accompany highly dramatic action, or for naturalistic tone-painting. It frequently preceded a great aria for one of the principal characters. The style of accompaniment varies widely: it may include simple, repeated or arpeggiated chords, tremolandos to underline high emotion, figures of accompaniment, fragmentary themes, or colourful illustrative music with obbligato instruments.

The use of accompanied recitative in Italian-language works increased steadily during the eighteenth century: for example, Haydn's own *opera seria Armida* (1784), as well as his oratorio *Tobia*, contains a number of richly-scored specimens. Non-Italian models existed in Mozart's *Die Zauberflöte* and in Handel's oratorios: *Messiah* contains a large number, some of which amount to free-form combinations of recitative and arioso, and *Joshua* even provides a representation of the sun and moon. It seems, however, that Haydn did not follow Handel's precedent closely in this particular genre (he may not have known *Joshua* at all). He had acquired an assured style and technique for writing accompanied recitatives relatively early in his career, and had no difficulty in applying it here, subject always to the adaptation of the melodic conventions to German or English prose.

As Smither has pointed out, recitatives in oratorio 'tend to include more descriptive and narrative qualities' than in opera, because of the absence of costumes, scenery and action.[3] In *The Creation* there is a very large descriptive element in the recitative texts, and Haydn and Swieten selected for obbligato treatment the ones containing the most lyrical descriptions of nature. These are Nos. 3, 12 and 21. Their texts are all poetic rather than biblical, and retain strong echoes of Milton; they were clearly designed to allow opportunities for musical illustration, and Haydn responded with alacrity. It was in these three movements that he incurred the strongest criticism for his 'Thonmalerey' (tone painting); and it was here also that he was able to indulge his bent for humour. This was a rare enough element in oratorio, though not unknown to Handel, for instance in his characterization of Polyphemus in *Acis and Galatea*.[4]

No. 3 portrays the 'elements': storms, clouds, rain, snow, and so on; No. 12 depicts the sun, moon and stars; and No. 21 singles out eight species of the animal creation. Haydn's general pattern is to present his musical picture of each element *before* the singer's words provide the key; this seems to have been a new idea of his own rather than, as Tovey claimed, 'the classical rule for the musical illustration of words'.[5] (It is difficult to find a clear precedent in any earlier work of Haydn or Mozart.[6]) In many cases the expected cadence after the singer's phrase is replaced by the beginning of the next illustrative passage. Most of the time the singer's part is merely conventional recitative (though in No. 21, bars 26–53, this has to be fitted into 6/8 time). The musical and pictorial interest and the humour are wholly in the orchestral accompaniment.

Haydn has the greatest fun with **No. 21**. He introduces the first three lines of text with a loud, not particularly illustrative phrase for unison strings – the kind of phrase found in many an operatic *scena*. A quiet repeat of this phrase[7] is interrupted by the roar of a lion on a low Ab for two trombones and contrabassoon with string trills, on a harsh third inversion of the dominant seventh (in some performances Haydn added the bassoons and bass trombone[8]), repeated on a Db in the middle of the recitative phrase. Simple upward 'slide' figures in the strings usher in the 'flexible tyger'. Then, with a change to 6/8, the 'nimble stag' and 'sprightly steed' make their appearance: here Haydn's music suggests rapid motion (he mercifully refrained from imitating the neighing horse).

The tonality has moved down by fifths from Bb to Db. Now there is an enharmonic shift to A, coinciding with a change of tempo, time signature and orchestration. All this is occasioned by the cattle and sheep, which Haydn signals not by a direct representation of the animals but by invoking the long-established pastoral convention. A flute, later joined by a bassoon, plays a serene, well-balanced melody in *siciliano* rhythm, with a quiet accompaniment for pizzicato strings. For once Raphael is invited to join in the fun, for the pause in bar 53 allows him, if he feels it is consistent with good taste, to offer a discreet imitation of 'bleating'. Before he has finished his phrase we hear the buzzing of approaching insects in a string tremolando (similar to the one used to depict the stars in No. 12). Last of all, 'In long dimensions creeps with sinuous trace the worm': an imposing final cadence of mock pomposity, preceded by a long slither for the cellos, whose meaning might have been guessed in advance of the text even by the first audiences.

The other accompanied recitatives serve different purposes. Those in Nos. 1 (bars 59–75) and 29, both following long orchestral introductions, paint moods rather than objects: chaos and tension in No. 1, pastoral serenity in No. 29; and their accompaniments use phrases from the preceding orchestral sections. At the same time each has an important modulating function. In both cases, and also in No. 12, the accompaniment turns into mere chords at the end as it prepares to introduce the following movement. No. 14 is merely a secco recitative orchestrated, no doubt with the object of providing loud chords to mark the beginning of Part Two.

The accompanied portion of **No. 16** is the only one of its kind. It is the one place where Haydn ventures to adorn the words of God himself with anything more than conventional accompanying chords. Swieten suggested: 'Here it seems that the bare accompaniment of the bass moving solemnly in a steady rhythm would create a good effect'. As we have seen, in an early sketch Haydn followed this suggestion, writing a secco recitative, but he later transfigured this with the present richly sombre scoring for divided violas and cellos, marvellously expressing the mysterious potency of the Creator. The strings move slowly and steadily through an independent, *stile antico* fantasia in D minor, on which Raphael's phrases are superimposed. Each of these phrases is in itself a conventional fragment of recitative, but in combination they have strong directional force, up to the climactic D and then down to A. It is worth noting how much more effective the melodic line is here when the English text is used (see Ex. 6). It avoids the over-repetition of the descending octave leap; it goes directly to the lowest note on the illustrated word 'deep'; and it permits an expressive crescendo on the word 'grow'. The contrast with the extroverted tone-painting recitatives is striking. No passage since before 'Let there be light' is more deeply religious in tone.

Arias and ensembles

Arias: No. **2** (with chorus), **4** (with chorus)[9], **6, 8, 15, 22, 24**
Duet: No. **32**
Trios: No. **18, 27**

The two-stanza aria text was well established in both *opera seria* and Italian oratorio before 1700, and in the early eighteenth century was almost always set in strict da capo form (ABA), the A section being in binary form with ritornellos. It was designed to reflect a single emotional state, or two complementary states expressed in the two stanzas.

Handel in his oratorios was most inventive in finding ways to abridge, interrupt or transform the da capo aria on an *ad hoc* basis, according to the dramatic situation. Often he brought the chorus into the scheme, as in 'Return, O God of hosts' in *Samson*. In two cases (Nos. 2, 4) Haydn did the same, but in general he does not seem to have followed Handel in his arias and ensembles. As with accompanied recitative, his own techniques and forms were already well set from his long experience in the writing of opera and, to some extent, oratorio.

In both operas and oratorios in the later eighteenth century the

Example 6 No. 16, bars 6–17

traditional da capo form was systematically modified in various ways; the process in oratorio has been thoroughly discussed by Howard Smither.[10] The most typical aria form in the classical period was one not unlike sonata-allegro form, and even closer to the first movement of a concerto. The first A section ended in the dominant or relative major key with new melodic material (a 'second subject'), while in the second A section the tonal scheme was modified to allow this material to return in the tonic. The B section, however, was less a 'development' than an exploration of contrasting moods and tonalities, as in the old da capo form. The ritornello framework remained, clearly distinguishing aria and concerto structures from actual sonata movements. Duets and trios, much less common than arias, generally followed the same forms. Highly regular examples of the transformed da capo form are 'Zeffiretti lusinghieri' in Mozart's *Idomeneo* and 'Quel felice nocchier' in Haydn's *Tobia*. In some instances the resulting structure is almost indistinguishable from an instrumental sonata first movement, and for this reason some writers speak of 'sonata-form arias'. There is no evidence, however, that opera or oratorio copied instrumental music; if anything the reverse is more likely, and the undoubted historical descent of this type of aria from the da capo aria can be clearly traced. I have therefore followed Smither in terming this a 'transformed da capo form'.[11]

A new type of formal aria was increasingly common for main characters in *opera seria* in the classical period: the *rondò* (its accent distinguishes it from the more familiar 'rondo'). It consisted of an Adagio, often ending on dominant harmony, followed by an Allegro in the same key or the parallel major. The Adagio has a main theme, moves away to related keys, and returns to the main theme in the tonic, which is generally then interrupted by the change of tempo. This form may have been an ancestor of the nineteenth century 'cavatina and caballetta'. It facilitated the dramatic exit, but also favoured a transition from calm to excitement, whether the emotion was love, rage or despair. Both Mozart and Haydn used the form frequently in their later operas: classic examples are 'Dove sono' in *Le nozze di Figaro* and 'Aure chete' in Haydn's *Orlando paladino*. It is also found in duets: 'Ah guarda, sorella' in *Così fan tutte*, 'Cara, sarò fedele' in Haydn's *Armida*; but in neither of these cases was the opening theme recapitulated in the tonic before the change of tempo.

Strophic forms were too popular in nature to be much used in *opera seria* or oratorio, but they were beginning to make their way into *opera buffa* and were, of course, quite at home in *Singspiel*.

Haydn clearly felt free to follow his own and Swieten's inclinations in composing arias and ensembles for *The Creation*. In any case, the texts provided by the libretto did not fall into the neat two-stanza pattern that had been the basis for conventional forms in earlier Italian and German oratorios. One can still see vestiges of the conventional forms in the arias and ensembles of *The Creation*, as we shall see in the examples below. But one factor tended to discourage musical recapitulation: the narrative element in the texts, with the many opportunities for tone-painting which Haydn seldom passed by. For instance No. 24 deals with the creation of man, then of woman; obviously one does not want to hear about man a second time. In No. 22 the text does divide roughly into two stanzas, but the second so clearly leads on to what follows that a da capo is out of the question. On the other hand the text of No. 27 happens to suggest ternary form, so Haydn uses a transformed da capo structure with new words for the third section. The text of the earlier trio, No. 18, suggests a strophic structure; Haydn sets the first two stanzas to the same music, but with added flourishes inspired by the words of the second; in the third, both the change to a bass voice and the subject matter induce him to provide new material.

The great tone-painting arias are No. 2 (the fall of the spirits of darkness), No. 6 (seas, mountains and rivers), and No. 15 (various birds). Illustrative arias about birds are a well-worn cliché of *opera seria*, and Haydn could be very sure of his ground in No. 15, but the painting is of the decorative order, superimposed on a rather traditional structure in which the main themes are innocent of tone-painting. In No. 6, by contrast, painting pervades the musical texture: 'the ornamental' and 'the beautiful' give way entirely to 'the sublime' (to adopt categories introduced by William Crotch[12]), and we are in the world of Turner's or Friedrich's landscapes.

No. 8 is a perfect example of the transformed da capo form (cognate with instrumental sonata form), as befits a wholly lyrical text that contains little contrast of image and none of mood (see Table 2). Outlines of the same plan are apparent in Nos. 4, 6, 15 and 27. In No. 4 ('The marv'lous work') not only is the opening text repeated, but the opening A section ends in the tonic (bar 22), which actually brings it closer to the old unmodified da capo form, despite the choral interpolations. In the imposing Trio, No. 27, the 'second subject' material of the first A section (bars 14–34) is freely transformed in the recapitulation (64–77, repeated 77–92): the parallelism here is most clearly seen in the harmony and rhythm of the opening phrases (14–16, 64–6) and of the cadential phrases (31–4, 74–7).

Table 2. Structure of 'With verdure clad' (No. 8)

Bars	Text lines	Section	Musical materials	Keys
Part One				
1–4	..	A	ritornello 1 (=beginning of A1)	Bb
4–16	1–3		A1	Bb
16–18	..		ritornello 2 (=beginning of A2)	Bb
18–36	4–6		A2+coloratura and cadence	Bb–F
36–8	..		ritornello 3 (concluding) and link	F
39–51	7–9	B		db–Db–Ab–bb–Bbv
52–3	..	A'	ritornello 1, abridged	Bb
53–65	1–3		A1	Bb
65–7	..		ritornello 2	Bb
67–87	4–6		A2+coloratura and cadence	Bb
87–9	..		ritornello 3 and final chords	Bb

In **No. 15** ('On mighty pens'), the most formal and elaborate aria in the work, the A section (depicting the eagle, lark and dove) ends on the dominant at bar 115 and is followed by a ritornello beginning in that key. The B section (introducing the nightingale) ends at bar 133 or bar 150, according to taste, but the two main melodic ideas that replace the A section after the return to the tonic (bars 151–5 and 164–6, representing the nightingale's tune) are anticipated not in the A section itself, but in ritornellos (19–22, 119–21).

In **No. 6** ('Rolling in foaming billows') the process is taken a step further away from direct recapitulation. As the text moves through the contrasting watery phenomena of seas, rivers and brooks (with mountain tops also making their appearance), Haydn is constrained to offer entirely new material for each, and even to switch to the parallel major for the lyrical final section. Yet the overall ternary structure of the transformed da capo form is still plainly seen in the tonal plan, with a 'second subject' in the relative major beginning at bar 28 and a modulating B section following the ritornello (beginning at 49), very much as in Table 2. Of course, it is the audience's familiarity with ternary structures that allows Haydn to establish their shadowy presence, and their attendant expectations, without actually repeating either the words or the music of the A section.

The same could be said about **No. 2** ('Now vanish before the holy beams'). 'A new created world' (bar 96) sounds like a recapitulation, returning to the positive mood and key of the opening text after the frightening glimpse of the fallen angels' despair; yet it is entirely new material. A balanced eight-bar tune sung twice instead of an open-ended 'aria' type of melody, it is sung by the chorus rather than Uriel, and it is allegro where the opening section was andante (possibly there is some influence of the *rondò* here). The feeling of recapitulation is not without thematic support, for the cadence of the new melody (bars 101–4) can be heard as a transformation of the dominant cadence of the first section (46–9). Before the movement ends Haydn returns to the 'despairing' music in shortened form, and then gives his 'new created world' tune twice more, the last time with a wonderful harmonic surprise (in bar 141).

Nos. 22 and 24 perhaps derive from the mid-eighteenth-century cavatina; at any rate they are best regarded as free binary structures. They begin with a ritornello introducing an opening vocal section that modulates to a new key, then proceed to an orthodox tonic recapitulation; but in both cases significant new text impels Haydn to depart from the original melodic material. In No. 22 ('Now heav'n in all her glory shone') the binary scheme is strongly reinforced by a transformed recapitulation of 'second subject' material in the orchestra (compare bars 82–6 with 45–50).

No. 24 ('In native worth') comments on the creation of man and woman, and Haydn charmingly distinguishes the sexes according to gender differences accepted in his time. The masculine qualities of Adam are reflected in the melody and texture of the A section, with its boldly chromatic harmonies at the climax (bars 20–1); when this section is recapitulated (beginning at bar 55) the opening phrase is the same, but the strong repeated-note chords of the accompaniment melt into a rounded legato over a tonic pedal (64–7), while Uriel sings a more sustained melody. On repetition this tune is adorned with some of Haydn's most delicious orchestral detail, and the cello line[13] emerges with a lyrical obbligato (see Ex. 7). The aria ends in a soft dream of beauty. This portrayal of woman is certainly sentimental. Like the text, the music reflects man's feelings about her rather than her actual character; but it is a superb example of Haydn's ability to fashion conventional forms to the needs of his text.

Conventional expectation is put to other use in the same aria. It contains the most extraordinary tonal surprise in the whole work – perhaps in all

Example 7 No. 24, bars 71–86

76

classical music – and the surprise depends for its effect on the strength of contrary expectation induced by the conventions of form. After a very strong and perfectly normal modulation and cadence in the dominant, G (bars 33–43), reinforced by a brief ritornello, Uriel begins what looks to be an ordinary repeat of the same passage, but by an astonishing twist Haydn diverts it to a cadence in Ab (see Ex. 8). He then calmly turns the Ab chord into an augmented sixth in C and proceeds at once to the recapitulation already described, as if nothing unusual had happened. No amount of rehearing of this amazing passage can make it sound ordinary. But I can think of no reason for it arising out of the text ('the breath and image of his God'), and I must conclude that it is simply an example of Haydn's well-known love of tricking his audience.

Example 8 No. 24, bars 32–51

The love duet, **No. 32**, is a *rondò* in its general character, though it lacks the clear tonic recapitulation near the end of the slow section that is a feature of orthodox examples. There are strong suggestions of *opera buffa* or *Singspiel*, well suited to the one episode where Adam and Eve show their humanity. The Adagio embodies Adam and Eve's formal opening statements of mutual love, he in the tonic, she echoing his melody in the dominant (the key relationship may indicate subordination, but it also suits the tessituras of the two singers, which are about one and a half octaves apart). They come together in a return to the tonic, and then follows the boisterous Allegro which, as Levarie points out, is not unlike an *écossaise*.[14] As before, Eve echoes Adam's phrases, but at a closer time interval, and this time in the subdominant. The music is heard twice through; the second time the concluding coloratura passages are taken over by the orchestra and there is a short coda. So we take leave of Adam and Eve singing and dancing their way through the Garden, watched benevolently by the angel Uriel ('O happy pair!', No. 33).

The Trio, **No. 18**, is one of the few movements with a strophic structure in its text (No. 30 is another). Each angel has a six-line stanza clearly divided into two three-line sentences, then they come together for a short coda. Haydn's setting reflects this form. After a long ritornello, Gabriel's and Uriel's verses are set to essentially the same music, ending on the dominant, except that Uriel's has extra wind figures to depict the birds. Raphael, without waiting for Uriel to finish, sings of the fish and of leviathan, naturally with new music, going through related keys to a cadence on D. Here the pulsating accompaniment at last ceases, and a soberly imitative section for all three angels brings the movement to a conclusion on the dominant. The whole structure is deftly tied together by a quiet orchestral figure (bars 11–14, 50–1, 127–31).

Choruses

No.10, **13**, 19, 26, 28, 34; the chorus also participates in No. **1** (see Accompanied Recitatives), Nos. 2 and 4 (see Arias and Ensembles) and No. 30 (see The Hymn, below)

It is in the choruses of *The Creation* that Haydn's debt to Handel is most obvious. The power of the older master reached him directly, over the heads of two generations of *galanterie*. The chorus had played no very prominent part in Viennese oratorio before his time, but already in *Tobia* he had shown greater interest in it than most of his contemporaries. His choral version of *The Seven Last Words* had been composed in 1796, shortly before he began work on *The Creation*, but it was merely an adaptation of a work conceived for instruments. The choruses of *The Creation* bring to fruition the seed sown by Handel's oratorios when Haydn had heard them in London.

Handel had used the chorus in diverse ways in his oratorios. Often, as in *Saul*, it is a protagonist, representing the people of Israel, whose destiny is closely bound up with the hero's; sometimes, as in *Samson*, it speaks for both sides in a tribal war; in *Hercules* it offers moral commentary, as a mere observer of events; in *Israel in Egypt* it is the chief narrator of a story of national heroism. In most of the biblical oratorios, and above all in *Messiah*, it is used at climactic moments to praise God.

In *The Creation* the chorus chiefly represents the Heavenly Host, called on to praise God at the end of the Third, Fourth, Fifth and Sixth Days, and at the end of the oratorio. In No. 30, treated separately below, the Host joins with Adam and Eve in the act of praise. Indeed, praise was probably the chorus's exclusive function in the plan of the original librettist. As we have seen, choral participation in the biblical narrative in No. 1, and in the descriptive commentary in Nos. 2 and 4, was most likely Swieten's idea; it happily gave Haydn some opportunity to emulate the vividness and drama of Handel's descriptive choral writing, above all in what some have regarded as his greatest stroke of genius, the 'Light'.

For this passage (**No. 1**, bars 76–89), Swieten's suggestion was as follows: 'In the Chorus, the darkness could gradually disappear; but enough of the darkness should remain to make the momentary transition to light very effective. "Es werde Licht &c." ["and there was Light"] must only be said once.'[15] Haydn did not follow this guidance. He showed the 'darkness' only by the keys of Eb and C minor, and perhaps by the quiet, staccato chords of the still muted strings. Then comes the Word of God. Handel, in the passage that most nearly resembles Haydn's ('Oh first created beam' in *Samson*), made this as impressive as the light itself (Ex. 9). Haydn has the Word sung quietly by the chorus together amid dead silence; the tension is such that you could hear a pin drop (and do, in the form of a pizzicato string chord). For the moment when light appears, Haydn has kept in reserve the key of C major, the unmuted strings in harsh double-stopping, and the entire wind, brass and timpani sections of the orchestra. The effect is of a simplicity that could only have been dared by a composer enjoying universal respect and admiration.

Example 9 Handel, *Samson*, No. 16 ('On first created beam'), bars 5–9

In six free-standing movements the chorus sings unbroken praise, without conflict or nuance and with little pictorial imagery. Inspired by Handel's example, Haydn triumphantly overcame this challenge to his creativity. To his habitual command of the orchestra and the language of classical music he added the majesty of 'learned' counterpoint and the naked force of diatonic block harmony. He combined these elements with Handelian freedom and seemingly inexhaustible variety. He also brought in the trio of angels, participating in Nos. 13 and 19 and providing contrast between the related choruses Nos. 26 and 28; and an unnamed quartet of soloists adds brilliance to No. 34.

Three of his choruses (Nos. 10, 28, 34) contain 'full dress' fugues, embedded in a homophonic framework. All are in a briskly energetic, major-mode common time, with themes using repeated-note quavers and with semiquaver coloratura passages. They recall 'For unto us a child is born' (*Messiah*) in mood, rhythm and texture, and this may have been one of Haydn's models, though it is not a fugue. The fugue in No. 10 includes, or at least suggests, most of the textbook devices: stretto, entries in related minor keys, augmentation and a cadential dominant pedal; and it follows Handel's habit of solidifying into homophony at the climax (bars 43–7).

No. 28 begins with the same text and music as No. 26, but whereas the earlier chorus had only a short fugato, it has a full double fugue, with double (bar 16) and even triple (44) parallel entries as well as simultaneous inversion (52), and the counterpoint keeps up almost to the end, leaving time only for the short, sharp cadences that are a trademark of Haydn's religious music. No. 34 is another, somewhat similar double fugue in the same key, Bb; one of its subjects has semiquaver passagework that blossoms into a coloratura section for the solo quartet before the huge, striding unisons that conclude the oratorio.

The most famous chorus (unless you include the 'light' passage in No. 1) is **No. 13**, the triumphantly extroverted conclusion of Part One. The text comes from Psalm ix.1–2 and 4; the form is most unusual and not entirely successful. It begins with a balanced melody, each half of which is repeated; the first half, carrying the phrase 'The heavens are telling the glory of God', is never heard again as such, although its text returns twice as a choral refrain separated by other lines. The beginning of the melody actually serves as the concluding cadence of the preceding recitative, and it is almost as if Haydn thought of it as belonging to No. 12.

Before the chorus is well established, the trio of angels comes in with a new melody; the notion of a day talking to another day evidently baffled even Haydn's tone-painting powers, but the passage from day to night is duly marked by a C major – C minor transition, coming too early in the movement for optimum musical effect. The second trio section is loosely based on the opening melody, extended with a comfortable-sounding cadence (bars 63–71); on repetition this is further lengthened by pauses (dangerously, in Tovey's opinion[16]). Each trio is followed by choral counterpoint based on the second part of the opening tune, and after a cadence on G a long fugato on the same upward scale figure begins (109).

The development through neighbouring keys sounds perfunctory, and before the end of the chorus we are going to become somewhat tired of the sopranos singing that upward scale figure in C major (which they do six times, at bars 42, 99, 115, 134, 145 and 167). Inverted entries fail to thrill, but the bass entry ending on a Bb (155) gives the first intimation of the coming grand conclusion. When it occurs again after a long dominant pedal, the Bb is held, and leads to an exhilarating series of chromatic modulations that drive invincibly to the final blaze of C major.

If Haydn's creative energy seems for once to flag in the course of this movement, it must be said that it has been a consistent favourite with English and American choirs. It was, of course, the concluding movement of the many performances of Part One only, which were probably more common than performances of the whole work in the nineteenth century. And the opening melody, obvious or even trite though it may be (one early reviewer pointed out that it closely resembled Theodore Hook's Vauxhall song, 'The Lass of Richmond Hill'[17]), has been the basis of more than one durable hymn tune.[18]

Orchestral movements

No. 1 (bars 1–59), 29 (bars 1–24)

The first and third parts of *The Creation* begin with musical introductions of quite different character and purpose. Part Three opens at a moment of idyllic repose. God is, presumably, resting after his labours; Adam and Eve are about to experience their first sunrise; 'from the celestial vaults pure harmony descends on ravished earth'. Haydn, in his element here, illustrates with a tonally stable, sweetly pastoral introduction in E major (No. 29). Inventively, he scored the opening tune for three flutes – his first idea was to leave them unaccompanied, but as an afterthought he supported them, first with a continuo part, and then with pizzicato strings, perhaps for security in performance.[19] (They are allowed to perform alone at bars 29–32.)

The Introduction to Part One, by contrast (**No. 1**), set Haydn possibly the greatest challenge of his career: nothing less than the Representation of Chaos in terms of that balanced and elegant classical idiom that he himself had done more than any other composer to develop. We know how much trouble he had with it from the fact that no less than seven sketches have survived. The final product has been more written about, perhaps, than any other piece of music so short, and has been described in wildly varying terms, ranging from 'an exceedingly unchaotic fugue'[20] to 'an instrumental movement in a bizarre motet style, a ricercar functioning as an *exordium*'.[21]

Haydn used the simplest possible means, a great unison C, to paint the void preceding creation: as Tovey put it, 'Here is your infinite empty space'. The sounds of the next few bars are certainly, by the conventions of 1800, so unusual as to deprive the audience of all power to predict their outcome, and hence to grasp their meaning; reassurance comes only with the bassoon triplet arpeggios in bar 6, after which one begins to know where one may be going. One soon realizes that whatever may occur along the way, Haydn is not going to make a serious structural departure from the normal symphonic adagios of his maturity. Charles Rosen accurately describes the movement as 'in "slow-movement sonata form" ', and adds: 'nothing could show better how, for Haydn, the "sonata" is not a form at all, but an integral part of the musical language.'[22]

The structure is blurred, but not completely hidden, by repeatedly denied expectations. At bars 6–8 we seem to be moving towards an imperfect cadence on the dominant (as actually occurs in the recapitulation, at 44), but the harmony turns to E♭ instead. At 16–19 we appear to be approaching a cadence on E♭, the likely complementary key of the movement, to confirm the modulation that is clearly taking place. But this is prevented by a wholly unexpected (though for Haydn by no means unprecedented) interruption in D♭ (21); again the cadence on E♭ is denied after 25–6, and yet again after 37–8, when it is conclusively evaded by the return to C minor. But there has nevertheless been an orthodox, if fragmentary, second subject in the relative major (28).

The recapitulation is easily recognized (40). It is 'telescoped', and now satisfies the expectations denied in the exposition; the second subject occurs in the tonic in combination with part of the opening material (50–3). The movement ends with a perfectly normal, if chromatically enriched, cadence in C minor.

What is 'chaotic' about this movement? The answer lies not in its form, but in numerous details: the vague and fragmentary themes, where more solid melodic material would normally appear (bars 3–5, 15–19, 28–31); unexpected touches like the uprushing wind scales (31, 39) and arpeggios (45–9); ambiguous harmonies (5–6, 9, 33, 37–8)[23]; above all, the denied expectations already mentioned. The composer himself, after playing over the movement to Silverstolpe, said to him: 'You have certainly noticed how I avoided the resolutions that you would most readily expect. The reason is, that there is no form in anything [in the universe] yet.'[24]

This, then, is how Haydn 'represented' chaos: by a refusal to meet the harmonic expectations that were the basis of classical style. While maintaining firmly the indispensable orderliness of his musical language, he used that language to denote disorder in this one striking but strictly limited respect. The harmonies themselves differ only in degree from some of his own precedents (the first movement of the String Quartet Op. 71 No. 3, the slow introduction to Symphony No. 97, the 'Et incarnatus est' of the *Missa in tempore bello*). But it would be several decades before any major composer would go further in chromatic ambiguity than Haydn did in the opening bars of 'Chaos'. That composer was Richard Wagner, whose 'Tristan chord' Haydn actually anticipates (in a different inversion and key) in bar 6.

To return, however, to the opening unison C, which comes before even the expectations are set up – before all things began. Why did Haydn choose this gesture to represent the most sublime? Symbolism does not supply a convincing answer, and it is difficult to believe that Haydn would have allowed arcane hidden meanings to govern his choices in a work that undeniably aimed to uplift the larger public. To my ears, the beginning of Haydn's 'Chaos' echoes that of Mozart's Fantasia in C minor for piano, K. 475 (1785), which may well have been the unconscious model for the whole movement; there are a number of parallels, shown in Ex. 10. Haydn had used opening unisons suggesting minor harmony before (e.g. in Symphonies 102 and 103), but the coincidence of key and the other resemblances do suggest a connection with the Mozart Fantasia – that precocious harbinger of brooding, Romantic gloom that rings through so many C-minor openings in nineteenth-century music. There is a further possible link with Mozart's C minor piano concerto, which shares the bare C unison opening and the prominence of the 'Neapolitan' key of Db major.

If, indeed, Haydn turned to Mozart rather than Handel for inspiration at this supreme moment in his creative life, it may have been because the younger composer's music had more deeply touched his personal religious feeling as opposed to his appreciation of grandeur. The awe-inspiring idea of a void before all time was akin to the contemplation of death and the eternal hereafter. It drew from Haydn the ominous language of Romanticism, not the enlightened optimism that could prevail as soon as Light had appeared. And what music, in the 1790s, was more Romantic than Mozart's?

The Hymn

No. 30

At the end of No. 29, the angel Uriel invites the Heavenly Host to join the newly made human pair in praise of their creator: 'Then let our voices ring united with their song'. The movement that follows for duet and chorus (**No. 30**) is the most substantial of the whole work, and is its summit: in Tovey's view 'the greatest thing in *The Creation* since the Chaos and the Light' and, more, 'the greatest movement, or pair of movements, that [Haydn] ever wrote, whether vocal or instrumental'.[25]

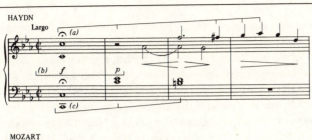

Note : *(b)*, *(e)* refer to the dynamic marks only

Example 10 Comparison of 'Representation of Chaos'
and Mozart's Fantasia, K. 475.
In this example the passages from *The Creation* are given in
Clementi's piano reduction (1800?).

Its original title was simply 'Hymn'. This survives in both the London librettos of 1800, and as 'Lobgesang' in the translation Swieten prepared for Haydn. Why it was deleted in the later sources, and by whose hand, we do not know, but it is a most appropriate description. Man and woman were created as intelligent beings so that they could return thanks to God (as we read in No. 22); now they perform this duty, supported by the angelic choir, before turning to their own pleasures (as we read in No. 31). They do so in a text that, unlike the rest, is in the common metre of English hymnody, with regular 'refrains'[26] in four-foot iambics for the angelic chorus.

The Hymn is a microcosm of the whole oratorio. Adam and Eve review the creation in detail, inviting each element to praise God, while the angels offer general praise at the end of each section. At bars 146 and 211 we see the human couple leading the angels in responsorial hymnody. The form somewhat recalls that of another great hymn, the *Benedicite omnia opera* ('O all ye works of the Lord, bless ye the Lord'). Table 3 shows how the strophic form of the hymn text relates to Haydn's setting.

The Adagio expresses the profound thankfulness of Adam and Eve for the 'bliss' in which they find themselves and their awe at first sight of the wonders of the world. Haydn uses a lyrical and spacious binary form, with Eve leading Adam in imitative entries. On the return of the main theme (bar 24) the chorus accompanies with a reverential call to praise, a block chant almost recalling *falsobordone*: it is enhanced by an extraordinary intermittent timpani roll that begins at bar 31 and lasts out the Adagio. The mood prevails with Adam and Eve in the hushed coda over a tonic pedal, which brings all to their knees. The subdominant harmony normal in such codas proves, in this case, to be a foretaste of the Allegretto, and the slow introduction is given the status of a prelude by the simple device of making its tonic the dominant of the following section.

The Allegretto is the most advanced example of one of Haydn's old favourites, the 2/4 rondo, surmounted by a climactic coda which returns to the key and mood of the Adagio, so that the overall plan is roughly ternary. His rondo theme (**A** in the table) is a binary tune, each strain first played and then sung, and the second strain repeated. After Adam has stated it the chorus sings a 'refrain' in the form of a brief fugato, climaxing in an emphatic unison phrase (bars 94–6) which might be called the 'shouts of praise' motive and is the link between the three **B** sections. The next episode (126–) is more contrasted, and faintly illustrative of the 'mists and steams'; it modulates to the flat side, and is followed by a 'refrain' firmly in Ab, with Adam and Eve leading the angels in their shouts of praise. In this

Table 3. Structure of the Hymn (No. 30)

Text verse	Singers	Subject	Bars	Musical material	Keys
1.	Eve, Adam	The world	1–47	*Adagio*: binary	C-G-C
R	chorus	praise	24–47	introduction	
2.	Adam	The sun	47–83	*Allegretto*	
				A ('rondo theme')	F
R	chorus	praise	82–97	B	F-Fv
3.	Eve	Moon and stars	97–125	A	F
4.	Adam	The elements	126–43	C	Bb-Abv
R	Eve, Adam, chorus	praise	144–61	B'	Ab
5.	Eve	Plant kingdom	160–94	A	Ab
6.	Adam	Animal kingdom	194–210	D	Ab-bb-Gb-ebv
R	Eve, Adam, chorus	praise	211–24	B''	eb-f-gv
7.	Eve, Adam	Nature to echo their praise	226–62	A extended	G
R	chorus	praise	263–90	E (slow homophony)	C-Cv
			290–332	F (fugato)	C-Cv
			332–43	E'	cv-C
			343–86	conclusion	C

'R' denotes the choral 'refrains' of general praise that follow most of the four-line common-metre verses, 'v' denotes dominant harmony.

new key the third statement of the rondo tune comes in, overlapping the cadence, with the addition of a bassoon an octave below the violin melody. Another episode takes the tonality still farther afield, to Eb minor, but it then climbs to G minor for more shouts of praise, ushering in the rondo tune, for the last time, in the unexpectedly bright key of G major with a flute in the higher octave.

Now Adam and Eve, together with their rondo melody, recede into the background, and the angels take centre stage for the brilliant coda. With no pause or change of tempo the music quickly returns to C major, where the angels sing a fervent 'Hail'; brass and timpani enter for the first time, enormously adding to the solemnity. Over an unremitting bustle of semiquavers in the strings there is a series of contrasts between the notions of adoring God and praising him (the contrast is perhaps clearer in German, where *beten* conveys the idea of prayer as well as adoration). In bars 276–90 the angels are bowed down in worship, and their slow homophony recalls their mood in the Adagio. But soon, at 'we praise thee', their energy bursts forth again in a brisk fugato, and at bar 325 Haydn illustrates 'evermore' by a combination of a long held G in three octaves accompanied by the inveterate semiquavers in the strings. At 332 the slow chanting returns. Three times a high shout of praise is followed abruptly by a low obeisance, the third taking the basses to a low F. Then at bar 370 the chorus rouses itself for the crowning acclamation.

7

Excerpts from critical essays

Carl Friedrich Zelter (1802)

From a review of the published full score in the *Allgemeine musikalische Zeitung* 4 (1801–2), cols. 385–96, attributed to Zelter by H. C. Robbins Landon. The translation is mine.

The poem is a collection of pictures taken from the works of nature, and passes by like a succession of images, experienced and developed by means of skilful musicianship. The subject is the biblical account of the creation of the world: the poet dwells on the principal elements of the story from time to time, adding his own comments. In other words, the text is a description that is both narrative and poetic ... To establish the necessary contrast, the poet has portrayed the absence of light and order as hostile forces, and has set against them the newly created light as a more powerful force. There is no place here for either persons or actions, and it is not clear why the poet has introduced the angels Raphael, Gabriel and Uriel to tell us the story of the creation as if they had been present. It is no excuse that these quite insignificant names lend plausibility to the variety of voices, for the poet could and should have represented the solo voices as he represents the chorus [that is, anonymously].[1] In short, so long as no character is revealed by actions and motivations, no person or name can be envisaged. We do not know whether the poet began with a theory for this oratorio; presumably he had a reason [for this decision], but it cannot be perceived. This apparently minor circumstance interferes with the clear comprehension of this excellent work, even for the keenest and most experienced music-lovers, who in their open enjoyment of the work are still unable to grasp its nature. So much for the poem; we will not dwell on it, for it is quite unsatisfactory throughout.

... The Overture bespeaks a master of the first rank, and is, in our opinion, the greatest section of the work: the crown on a royal head. It is called Representation of Chaos. With almost all possible instruments available as raw materials, a gigantic, almost incalculable web of artistic splendour is woven and formed. The objection that chaos cannot be depicted by means of harmony, melody and rhythm now falls to the ground, exposed as a crafty self-deception, by which a composer can if need be excuse himself for failing to solve such a problem. Despite the appearance of impossibility and of contradiction, this marvel (*Fabelhaftigkeit*) is in fact the most poetic and hence the best part of the whole plan, and our master has expounded it in a truly poetic, rich and original fashion. Abundant luxury of chords, figures and passages reigns here, such as a musical prince might display, with oriental splendour, for the ear and taste of his most distinguished guests – a treasure of genius and craftsmanship spread out for their delectation, rising out of the depths like the morning sun. . . .

Almost all discords that occur are deliberately treated with complete freedom. The unusual combination of figures and note-lengths, which include semibreves, minims, crotchets, quavers and semiquavers, triplets, roulades, trills and grace notes, gives the score a peculiar and mysterious look. One is astonished at the multitude of small, playful figures that swarm round huge dark masses, like clouds of insects against the great horizon. All these things in combination, in the dark imagery of chaos, make up an endlessly harmonious fabric, in which the succession of modulations is indescribably beautiful and in many places so sublime and lofty as to evoke awe.

It would be against the order of things, indeed impossible, for such a masterpiece to be universally recognized for what it is. There are deeply rooted theories, extracted from the music of the past, that always resist the spirit of progress. Naturally they give rise to a type of criticism that constantly demands but never congratulates. Such criticism must of course be carefully prevented from breaking its branches on such a work as this overture. That, too, is natural.

After the Overture, the creation story unfolds in biblical sequence, divided into the customary succession of recitatives, arias and choruses. The recitatives, as straight narrative, afford no opportunity for lyrical expression, and are therefore quite freely treated by the composer. Most of them are furnished with instrumental accompaniments, not so much according to the feeling and sense of the subject as to the literal meaning of the words. They deserve close attention for the masterly orchestration and the great variety of invention, which seems to pour out as if by chance (*wie von Ohngefahr*). The arias, on the other hand, are much more structured, although the narrative continues in them, too: and here we find an incompatibility between composer and libretto. The first aria is as follows: ['Now vanish before the holy beams', etc. – the German text quoted in full]. If the poet intended these words for an aria, he misunderstood the nature of the genre. An aria must be set in the present time, both in name and in fact; it can be permitted to encompass the past or the future only insofar as these can be regarded from the point of view of the present.[2] But if the composer needed to have an aria here, at least the words of the narrative should not have been repeated. Who wants to hear a story-teller repeating himself so often, interrupting the flow which alone maintains the interest of the story? The delight which this aria arouses every time it is heard is entirely due to the composer, who despite the narrative character of the text conveys a genuine feeling of immediacy, suggesting the bright morning of the first day, when night and confusion have been driven out by light and order – a new world observed and explained by itself. Then the chorus with its fugal texture makes a splendid entry. The metrical treatment of the ensuing text, '*Und eine neue Welt*' ['A new created world'], is of great beauty.

What has been said above concerning the organization of the recitatives and the first aria applies to most of the arias and recitatives in this oratorio.[3] In our opinion, they all have the same defect, which is covered up by the innumerable and conspicuous touches of genius on the part of the composer, both in melody and harmony. They excite admiration so long as one does not look at the words.

The passage in which the moon appears [No. 12] has a stirring, yearning beauty, and it is a pity that this gentle impression is immediately destroyed by what follows. The poet had a great opportunity here to develop some beautiful ideas out of the general concept of the quiet moon. He should have done his cutting where the subject matter is something less important than light.

The first aria of Part II [No. 15, 'On mighty pens'] is in every respect the most beautiful of the work. True, the composer had only to treat the poet's words as a painter would; true also, the eagle's flight and the dove's cooing cannot in themselves arouse any special pleasure. But [the depiction of the nightingale, bars 126–99] shows a purity and innocence which are praise-worthy beyond our powers of expression. The vocal line, indeed the whole score, at the words '*Noch drückte Gram nicht ihre Brust*' ['No grief affected yet her breast'] reminds one painfully of a state of innocence and integrity whose loss must sadden a sensitive soul. One sees with the highest admiration how the composer seizes every opportunity of using his art to express all that it can and will express.

The aria '*Nun scheint in vollem Glanze ...*' [No. 22, 'Now heaven in all her glory shines'] is a most melodious, grand and broad description of the magnificence of the newly created universe. The orchestration is exceptionally powerful and splendid: the horns and trumpets, especially, are handled with consummate mastery. The prayer '*Zu dir, O Herr! ...*' [No. 27, 'On thee each living soul awaits'] is partly accompanied by winds alone, with admirable fluidity throughout. In this respect it is recommended as a model for talented young composers.

And now, towards the end of Part II, man appears: and at last, in Part III, he and his wife enthuse over God's work, but unfortunately much too late, and in an insipid manner that detracts from the wonderful music.

We proceed to the choruses. If our composer was hitherto in his own terrain, he is now right at home. Almost without exception the treatment of the choruses is fugal. The subjects are memorable, and the answers and countersubjects enter freely and naturally. There is never any obscurity or confusion, and even the augmentations are clear and strong, though never pedantic. The treatment of the text is truer and bolder than in the arias and recitatives, while the orchestration throughout is excellent beyond description. Of special interest are the two choruses '*Denn er hat Himmel und Erde bekleidet*' [No. 10, bars 11–56, 'For he the heavens and the earth has clothed'] and '*Vollendet ist das grosse Werk*' [No. 26, or, more probably, No. 28, 'Achieved is the glorious work']. The theme of the former is a model fugue subject both from an expressive and a technical point of view: despite the verbal length of the phrase, it is both noble and clear. Eager young composers may have noticed that all the fugal choruses are light, supple and free, and that in all this great work there is not a single strict fugue. Let them be warned that such ease and freedom are possible only for someone who knows how to write a strict fugue with all its trappings . . . . Among Haydn's unforgettable merits is this: his excellent compositions, with all their fire, their truth and their zest, owe much to his fine use of counterpoint and to his fugal technique. The man who has left all his contemporaries behind him, with all his genius and his eternally fresh and youthful richness of invention, is not ashamed to adorn his works with contrapuntal beauties. As a result, despite all the changes of time and fashion, they will remain immortal so long as music lives.

William Gardiner (1811)

From a letter in defence of modern music published in *The Monthly Magazine* (London) for 1 March 1811 (vol. 31, pp. 133–6), signed 'W. G., Leicester, 1814'. The author was undoubtedly William Gardiner, the Leicester hosier, amateur musician and writer.

To exemplify what has been stated, we must open that treasure of musical sublimity, the Oratorio of the Creation. Here we find every voice and instrument conspiring to raise the mind of man to contemplate the wonderful work of God. . . .

The exquisite feeling in the songs, and the taste displayed in the accompaniment, exceeds in beauty every thing we have hitherto felt or conceived. The collision of the trumpets and trombones, and the awful motion of the bass, render the chorusses terrific and grand. The concluding movement of *The heavens are telling the glory of God* [No. 13, bars 95–196?], is penned with a majesty of thought that transcends the powers of musical expression. With our present means we can scarcely produce a shade of what the imagination of the musician would intend.

The volume of sound that is wanted in the bass, and that is requisite to give an amplitude of idea, must be sought for in instruments as yet unknown. Were it necessary to bring farther illustrations of the great powers of the new music compared with that of the antients, we might attempt a description of the chaos, which opens the work we have been quoting. It commences with all the known instruments, displayed in twenty-three distinct parts. After these are amalgamated in one tremendous note, a slight motion is made perceptible in the lower[4] parts of the band, to represent the rude masses of nature in a state of chaos. Amidst this turbid modulation, the bassoon is the first that makes an effort to rise and extricate itself from the cumbrous mass [bar 6]: the sort of motion with which it ascends, communicates a like disposition to the surrounding materials: but this is stifled by the falling of the double basses and the contrafagotto.[5]

In mingled confusion the clarinet struggles with more success [31?], and the etherial flute escapes into air [39?]. A disposition verging to order is seen and felt, and every resolution would intimate shape and adjustment, but not a concord ensues! After the volcanic eruptions of the clarini [trumpets] and trombones [40?], some arrangement is promised; a precipitation follows of the discordant sounds, and leaves a misty effect that happily expresses the '*Spirit of God moving upon the face of the waters*'

[76–80]. At the fiat, '*Let there be light!*', the instruments are unmuted, and the audience is lost in the refulgence of harmony. . . .

Thomas Busby (1819)

From his *General History of Music* (London, 1819), vol. 2, pp. 399–400.

[After Haydn returned to Vienna in 1795] he was now easy, and at leisure to enter upon a work at length. The majestic strains of Handel were still thundering in his ear, and he had two reasons for wishing to compose a second oratorio: first, the laudable ambition would be gratified, of aspiring to, or contending with, the sublimity of his great countryman; secondly, he would, by even a moderate imitation of such solid grandeur, obliterate the remembrance of his former failure in that province of composition. It was scarcely yet forgotten, but soon might be, that his *Tobias*, produced in 1774, was not a very splendid performance.[6] At the age of sixty-three, he commenced what he evidently intended for his greatest work. At the end of 1795 he began his oratorio of the *Creation*, and at the beginning of 1798 completed the undertaking, saying, 'I have spent much time over the piece, because I intended it should last'. In the succeeding Lent it was performed, for the first time, at Schwartzenberg Palace, at the request and expence of the *Dilettanti* Society. It was received, says a writer, who tells us he was present, with the most rapturous applause; and I can easily believe him; because the audience were unacquainted with the sublime loftiness, and profound contrivance of Handel, and went to the Schwartzenberg Palace with ears and minds prepared to be enchanted. But what are the real and prominent features of the composition? A series of attempted imitations of many things inimitable by music, the sudden creation of light happily expressed by an unexpected burst of sound, airs not abundantly beautiful or original, smothered with ingenious accompaniments, and choruses in which the composer toils under his incumbent weight, labours in fugue, copies with a faint pencil the clear lustre of a glorious prototype, and supplies the absence of true taste and dignity, with the congregated powers of a complicated band.* My respect for the great talents of Haydn obliges me to be sorry that his judgment did not forbid his compromising himself in

---

* If in any one of the melodies of the *Creation*, I could discover the celestial grace of Sacchini, in the recitatives the profound science of Sebastian Bach, or in the choruses, a single example of that transcendent force of imagination, profound adjustment of parts, or sublimity of aggregate effect, so uniformly conspicuous in Handel, I would allow Haydn to be an oratorio composer.

oratorial composition. In his operas and cantatas, his failure was only partial; in his oratorios, almost total. . . .

Edward Taylor [?] (1834)

From an unsigned review of the performance on 24 June 1834 as part of the Royal Musical Festival in Westminster Abbey, published in *Musical Library: Monthly Supplement* I (1834), p. 56. Leanne Langley, in a personal communication, has suggested Taylor as the likely author. In the performance under review there were 636 musicians taking part. The concert began with Handel's 'Zadok the priest', continued with *The Creation* with few if any cuts, and ended with a selection from Handel's *Samson*.

The *Creation* is an unequal work. The first part shines in all the splendour of Haydn's genius; but it is evident that the composer has here almost exhausted himself by the greatness of his efforts. In the second, his fire is not quite burnt out, and some of his invention remains, as is witnessed in the terzetto, and in the airs, 'Now heaven,' and 'In native worth' [Nos. 18, 22, 24]. But in the third, only the duet, &c., beginning 'By thee with bliss,' [30] bears the impress of the composer. The few bars of instrumental music at the opening [of No. 29] are most graceful, but this is their greatest praise. The nature of the subject has in a great measure led to this. After the creation of the firmament, the sublime, poetically and musically speaking, ceases. The second part, as it concerns the composer, only described what is great. And the third, which may be called domestic, is a representation of connubial happiness, of perfect contentment, and pious gratitude. Thus, so far as relates to musical effect – that is, the grandeur of it – the musician may be said to have had an anti-climax to work on. Nevertheless, in the last chorus, he ought to have put forth more strength. He appears to have been in haste to complete his work, and not to have allowed himself time to end it in the mighty manner in which it commences.

We did expect, on such an occasion, – the whole court, the bench of bishops, nay, many of the first literary characters of the age, forming part of the audience, – that the English version of this oratorio would have undergone further revision. Some of the alterations made from time to time were adopted, but much remained that is ludicrous and vulgar. It is discreditable to the taste of a nation to listen to anything so stupid, so monstrous. The directors probably relied upon a musical committee for the correction of all this. If so, let them next hope to gather grapes from brambles.

P.L.A. (1846)

From 'Beitrag zur Charakteristik J. Haydns', signed 'P.L.A.', in the *Neue Zeitschrift für Musik* 24 (1846), I, pp. 207–8. The translation is mine.

... I cannot explain to myself by any reasoning how it is possible that Haydn's surpassing greatness can have remained completely unrecognized in Vienna, where he had lived and formed himself in his youth. Only after he had travelled to London with the sagacious Salomon, and had returned to Vienna laden with triumphs and riches, did the Viennese, encouraged by the English, treat Haydn with respect. After the performance of his *Creation* – certainly a great, but by no means a flawless oratorio – they were driven with them [the English] to complete idolatry. But unfortunately this recognition came too late, long after he had produced his excellent and thitherto largely neglected works, including above all his excellent chamber compositions, whose light, clear and flowing melodies and unaffected, organic part writing ensure them an eternal spring. ... He was less happy in his compositions for the church. His fresh, often childish humour, and the humble position he took as a muscial aesthete (*musikalischer Aesthetiker*), made it difficult for him to avoid giving his serious compositions a worldly flavour: the oratorios are an appropriate example. The *Seven Last Words* in its original form is the one religious composition which is controlled and dignified in its execution from beginning to end. And yet the public has never made so much fuss of it as it has of *The Creation*, which is inferior in poetic value. The wild applause which was accorded to *The Creation* on its performance [in 1808] soon cost the old composer his life, for he was so overcome that he had to be carried from the concert room and revived. ...

George Alexander Macfarren (1854)

From an analytical essay published with a libretto for the Sacred Harmonic Society dated February 1854 (London: Published by the Society, [1854]).

[From the Preface]
When writing the *Creation*, [Haydn] would never enter upon the task of composition without first praying to be empowered to praise God worthily.

With, however, all his devout enthusiasm, Haydn was no puritan; religion was the joy of his heart, and not the sackcloth of his loins. Being charged with too light a style in his ecclesiastical music, and too cheerful an expression, 'Whenever I think of God,' said he, 'I can imagine only a Being infinitely great and infinitely good; and the idea of this latter attribute of the heavenly nature fills me with such confidence, with such joy, that I should set even a *Miserere* to cheerful music.'[7] In this speech I find the clue to the entire character of his sacred music; in this the justification of all that is at variance with the more prevalent style adopted for religious subjects. Whether in sacred or in secular subjects, an artist, to be natural and not pedantic, must write from the heart and not from convention; thus only can he give true expression to his feelings – thus only appeal with sincerity to the sympathies of others.

To judge the *Creation* by the composer's own principle – to trace in it his purpose – to hear it with his feelings, we must understand it to be a Hymn of Praise, a Song of Thanksgiving, the outpouring of 'confidence and joy'. They are, possibly, not our feelings which are embodied, but Haydn's; and, to do ourselves justice and the author, we must, for the time, identify ourselves with him – share his holiday of the heart, and feast at his festival of love; believing with him that the beauty of Heaven is not only on the other side of the horizon: let us assume this, and we shall enjoy his music all the more, and love our neighbours none the less for the assumption. As a work of art, the *Creation* is of a lighter character than any other sacred composition that has received the suffrages, not to say excited the enthusiasm, of the world; as a piece of expression, the speech I have quoted essentially translates its meaning, and it is useless for popular vocalists, and other arbiters of public taste, to attempt to pervert this meaning into one of seriousness and self-sacrifice, by drawling the tempo of some of the most spirited pieces, and thereby substituting dulness for devotion....

[From the notes to No. 2, 'Now vanish before the holy beams']
There is somewhat of abruptness in the commencement of this piece without harmony to determine the tonality in a key that is certainly remote from that in which the last concluded, although, indeed, not unrelated to it. Once passed the abrupt effect of its commencement, and the general character induced by the extreme change of tonic is fresh, and bright, and glowing, and thus appropriate to the words. The digression into the key of C minor, comprised in the vocal solo from the words 'Dismay'd the host of hell's dark spirits' [bar 53] (forming that irregular and broken succession of

declamatory phrases that, very commonly in modern operatic music, separates the Andante of an Air from the chief melody of the Cabaletta or principal Allegro, and is technically described as the Tempo di Mezzo,) – this digression is into a key so remote from the original and chiefly prevailing key of A major, as to startle, if not shock, the cultivated ear by its irrelative and uncongenial effect, and is not justifiable to the principles of musical propriety by the exigencies of verbal expression, which, however exacting they be, and entirely despotic as they are, may always be fulfilled by natural and coherent progressions. The graceful fluency of the two principal themes of this piece [beginning at bars 1 and 96] ... betokens such spontaneous ease of production, as can only be coincident with a composer's happiest mood: when we consider, therefore, Haydn's knowledge of the principles of musical construction, – knowledge so perfect and so familiar, that in his exercise of it in their application he seems to command them to his purpose, – when we consider this, and remember, that though he produced often rapidly, he wrote never hastily, we may all wonder at such a discrepancy as exists in the design of this piece; and the more we wonder, the less we admire. For my part, I cannot but think that an examination of the manuscript would disclose some change of the first intention, – some transposition of this piece, induced by circumstances such as the compass of the original singer's voice, or other like extraneous necessities, that might account for, if not vindicate, the peculiarity under consideration. . . .

Hugo Wolf (1885)

From a review of a performance of *The Creation*, published in *Salonblatt* (Vienna), 15 November 1885. Translation by Henry Pleasants, *The Music Criticism of Hugo Wolf* (New York and London, 1978), pp. 164–5, reprinted here by permission of Holmes and Meier Publishers, Inc.

'The Creation' by Haydn. What a spirit of childlike faith speaks from the heavenly pure tones of Haydn's music! It is the mark of his greatness as an artist that when we hear his music we are utterly unaware of the art, and yet what a variety of musical structures encloses his charming tonal pictures!

His extraordinarily keen artistic perception is most conspicuously evident in the field of tone painting, much cultivated in recent times, and now falling into disrepute. And, indeed, we would shudder at the very thought of what a modern composer might do in the handling – or mishandling – of a subject offering such opportunities for tone painting as 'The Creation' or 'The Seasons'. There would be so much depiction that we would hear no music. If a modern composer wished, for example, to illustrate chaos, it is certain that we would encounter no triad, unless possibly an augmented one. It would probably fall to a perfect fifth to defray the musical expenses of such a vision.

(If we could suppose that the good Lord had consecutive fifths ringing in his ears at his first glimpse of chaos, then it would follow that justified self-defense rather than wantonness or malice, as some philosophers have suggested, prompted his desperate decision, in the ridiculously short span of seven days, to inflict so much evil on the world. An ordinary piece of cotton wool to be sure, could have rendered the same service, but there were no trees at that time, nor plantation owners. The cotton wool industry still dreamt peacefully in the womb of chaos, and Jaeger shirts rightly were still a chimera. O, happy days of chaos!)

Still, one could live with this diabolical expressive device if only that had been the end of it, for today dissonances and shrill instrumental effects fall like hail about our ears, and the orchestra moans and groans until one is ready to believe that chaos has become a wild beast with a toothache. . . .

How different was Haydn's procedure. Just look at chaos in his 'Creation'. The very first measures, with the muted violins, awake in us the sensation of being in the presence of a mysterious something. A magician, he evokes the sombre picture of chaos. Gray fogbanks roll slowly on in disordered masses, illuminated by irridescent lights. Listen! What manner of voices are those, cries of distress and despair, gently solemn strains? They intertwine, dissolve, melt away. Another apparition emerges from the darkness, radiant in magical beauty [bar 22?]. The soul thrills at the sight of this enchanting phantom. With serene movement it pursues its course. It drifts upward. The atmosphere is suffused with deep red. It falters, falls – a flash of lightning out of the black abyss – and the apparition has vanished. Seas of mist again envelop the richly coloured scene. The tone poet has awakened from his dream.

That is, to be sure, a pitiful sketch compared with the fantastic world conjured up by the tone poet in his prophetic vision. But had Haydn wished to turn into music exactly what he had seen, one may assume with reasonable certainty that his chaos would have remained the more unintelligible in just the same degree that it speaks the more intelligibly to us now. Why? Because the composer has given us not his vision, but rather the impression made by the vision on his musical sensibility. . . .

Paul Dukas (1904)

From an essay, 'Haydn et Berlioz', dated 'Janvier 1904', in *Les écrits de Paul Dukas sur la musique* (Paris, 1948), pp. 604–7. Translation mine.

Haydn, like Berlioz, believed in the descriptive power of music, in the analogies between colours and timbres, and in the associations of ideas that transform literary or pictorial experiences into music. His art certainly seems the more naïve to us; what he attempted seems more honest or, if you like, more innocent. There is in his work neither weeping nor gnashing of teeth, and the romanticism which reigns there is that of a carefully tended English garden. Apart from certain passages of deliberate oddity, and of a boldness whose edge has not been blunted by the passing of a long century – I am thinking of the 'painting' of Chaos at the beginning of *The Creation* – Haydn always made his musical descriptions fit into classical form, and used for his 'tableaux' only the normal vocabulary of sonata, string quartet or symphony. That is what distinguishes him from Berlioz, who gave poetic expression precedence over musical, and modelled the latter on the former, applying to pure music the procedures of dramatic music. But even if these fundamental differences do not restrict the comparison in principle, one should not push it too far. Haydn, however much he believed in the descriptive power of music, believed even more strongly in its autonomous power, its absolute expressive value: he was descriptive only by way of a *jeu d'esprit* and as a diversion. Berlioz, on the contrary, was incapable throughout his life of writing a line of music without a text or a programme.

Heinrich Schenker (1926)

From 'Haydn: Die Schöpfung, Die Vorstellung des Chaos', in his *Das Meisterwerk in der Musik*, vol. 2 (Munich 1926), pp. 159–70. Translation mine.

The notion of Chaos is inseparably bound up with the coming of light and life: to see permanent non-fulfilment in Chaos is, itself, too chaotic a way of thinking. Therefore music, as an art that unfolds through time, is well placed to represent Chaos: the first rumblings and movements, the first stirrings of dark forces, the act of becoming, of giving birth, at last the light, the day, the creation!

But only by severe means can art express Chaos!

So Haydn, even for the Representation of Chaos, submits to the fundamental principles of his art; but he takes pains to expand and stretch his technique so far that one is reminded, by his riddles, of the riddle of Chaos itself.

(Bar 1) The first impulse – an initial *forte*: the octave emerges, movement begins.

(Bar 2) Consequence of the first impulse: the minor third appears in the violas (eb^1). Important as it is for Chaos to establish its minor mode at the outset, light will oppose it with its major mode. In the second half of the bar, however, ab^1 enters (Vln. 2) in place of the fifth of the triad: a $\frac{5}{3}$ chord must be gradually wrested from Chaos.

(Bar 3) The lowest voices fall a semitone, producing a suspension of ab^1, which increases the weight of the progression (*Tonfolge*) ab^1–g^1; the aural impression becomes a visual one (*das Ohr wird förmlich zum Auge*) (Ex. 11).

Example 11

An undulation above and below, the semitone steps being waves, the semibreve their wavelength: and the swell ($<$ $>$) proper to a suspension shares in the wave motion.

To the $\frac{7}{3}$ on the downbeat of bar 3 a fifth is added, f^2 (Vln. 1).

(Bar 4) The eb^2 expected in bar 4 is delayed to bar 5, as if its initiative were exhausted; g^2 represents an embellishment of the resolution [of f^2 to eb^2], and the crotchets ab^2–g^2, while establishing the high point [of the phrase], also form a diminution of the basic suspension motive ab^1–g^1.

(Bar 5) A second impulse: the *forte* carries forward the eb^2 resolution; again eb^1 and ab^1 appear – so the $\frac{5}{3}$ is still wanting, although the composing-out has clearly followed this objective (c^1–g^1–eb^1 in bars 2, 3, and 5).

As anticipated in bar 4, ab^2 also appears as reinforcement (Fl. 1, 2). Unlike bar 2, bar 5 is not divided by a tone entering on the upbeat, though here also ab is tied over [into the next bar].

(Bar 6) With the resolution of the suspension we return to motion in minims. The second oboe takes over ab^2 from the flute and thus moves into the reinforcing 9–8 relationship to the g^1 of the middle voice.... In return the flutes trade b with the cellos, thus paving the way for an inversion of bars 2–3:

ab^1–g^1	[becomes]	c^3–b♮^{2}
c^1–b♮^{1}		Ab–G

In the first half of the bar the 1st violin inserts f♯², in order to avoid a bare repetition (compare f²–eb² in bars 3–5); moreover, f♯² does not go to g², because this sequence (*Folge*) has already occurred between bars 3 and 4. The basic motive is formed for the fourth time by the tying over of ab². The bassoon plays the root, G, of the continuing chord. The first triplets come to life. The tying over of f² by the 1st violin again brings a < > with it.

(Bar 7) b² is also included in this tie, and goes to c³ in the second half of the bar.

(Bars 8–9) The inversion of bars 2–3 is now presented, with c³ over a bass Ab. The basic motive, Ab–G, is in the bass, stirring up the depths. For the first time Ab is not tied over, because of the syncopation of the c³.

To complete the inversion of bars 2–3, the possible continuations from c³ in the first half of the bar are shown in Ex. 12. The c³ could proceed as in (*a*) to b♮² (compare the movement of the cellos in bars 2–3), but a half cadence cutting in like that would have immediately lowered the tension; more satisfactory, then, is to proceed as in (*b*) or (*c*). And this is the route actually taken by the phrase. But it is the middle parts that move to bb (Cl.1, Fag. 1, 2): in their first notes eb¹–d¹ the connection with the viola's eb¹–d¹ in bars 2–3 and 5–6 is established. Meanwhile c³, taking advantage of the freedom of its status as a consonance despite being tied over (a third from the bass), moves emphatically to d³ (*sforzando*) and finally advances to eb³: the original shape is stretched out! The trumpets and drums join in celebrating the great moment; the dynamics increase (*p, f, sf,* <).

Example 12

The sequence (*Folge*) c³–d³–eb³ in bars 8–9 (Fl. 1, 2, Trb. 2) is the first melodic passage in Chaos, the first third-progression motive! Raphael utters this very same first motive from Chaos in his opening words; the two third-progression motives c–d–eb coincide (Ex. 13).

Example 13

In retrospect we understand the function of the $^6_3$ in the second half of bar 7: not only is the $^5_3$ chord avoided thereby, but also its consonance has appropriately demarcated the syncopated resolution b♮^{2}–c^3 from the third-progression motive.

In the second half of bar 8 the 2nd oboe and 2nd clarinet play f♯^{2} instead of f^2: f^2 would have stressed the B♭ chord more than necessary and thus produced the illusion of a IV–V–I [cadence] in E♭ major.

Donald Francis Tovey (1934)

From a programme note printed for a concert of the Reid Orchestral Concerts at the University of Edinburgh, 1 February 1934. The source for the text below is No. CCVI of the collected *Essays in Musical Analysis*, vol. 5 (London, 1937), pp. 114–46. It is reprinted here by permission of Oxford University Press.

The time is ripe for a better understanding of Haydn's *Creation* than can be inculcated by fashion. The reasons why it was out of fashion at the end of the nineteenth century are both obvious and obsolete; but they are much the same as the reasons which may now bring it into fashion again. When fashions are in revolt against the sublime and the romantic, Haydn may become fashionable, like Mozart, for the wrong reasons: that is to say, he is only too likely to become patronized by people who see in him exactly what the Philistine of the eighties saw who wrote in the first edition of *Grove's Dictionary* that Haydn, in his *Creation*, 'represents Chaos by means of an exceedingly unchaotic fugue'. It is better to risk losing such patronage than to lose what Haydn's contemporaries appreciated in him: the elements of the sublime and the romantic. Haydn's representation of Chaos is not a fugue; but the Chaos he intends to represent is no mere state of disorder and confusion. He has a remarkably consistent notion of it, which harmonizes well enough with the Biblical account of the Creation; not less well with the classical notions of Chaos, whether in Hesiod or Ovid; but most closely with the Nebular Hypothesis of Kant and Laplace, which almost certainly attracted Haydn's attention.[8] Kant's speculations on the subject had already been published in 1755, and Laplace's discussion of it was published in a readable and popular form in 1796, two years before Haydn's *Creation*. Haydn, who did a certain amount of dining out in *fin-de-siècle* London, was as likely to have heard of the Nebular Hypothesis as a modern diner-out is likely to hear of Einstein and Relativity. Moreover, he visited Herschel at Slough, saw his famous forty-foot telescope and his less famous but more successful other telescopes, and doubtless had much conversation with Herschel in German on both music and astronomy, Herschel having been a musician before he made astronomy his main occupation. Moreover, on May 3rd, 1788, Herschel published in the *Star and Morning Advertiser* a poetic 'Address to the Star' welcoming Haydn to England in glowing astronomical terms.[9] Be this as it may, the evolution of Cosmos from Chaos might be taken as a 'programme' of a large proportion of his symphonic introductions for many years before he achieved its grandest illustration with recognized and confessed purpose.

The text of the *Creation* is founded, at several removes, on *Paradise Lost*, and more especially on the account given to Adam by the 'affable archangel' in Book VII. Haydn is much more likely to have heard of the Nebular Hypothesis than to have read Milton. His librettist, the Baron Van Swieten, did not give him Milton's phrase 'loud misrule of Chaos', and this is just as well, for the work has nothing to do with the fiery ocean into which the rebel angels fell, and Haydn's symphonic nebular hypothesis is much more musical, as well as more universal. Being an artist, Haydn represents Chaos in a thinkable aspect; that is to say, he chooses a moment at which the evolution of Cosmos begins. Here is your infinite empty space. [Music example: No. 1, bar 1.] Strictly speaking, this mighty unison is the most chaotic part of the introduction. A significant chord would obviously be as futile a symbol of Chaos as an armchair; and a violent and unexplained discord would, even in modern music, be a mere phenomenon of human petulance. Classical tonality is Haydn's musical Cosmos, and modern atonality represents, as the modern composer is beginning to find out, a much narrower range of possibilities. So Haydn, like Herschel, proceeds to explore the musical universe with higher and higher powers of his telescope. And, while Herschel arrives at remarkably sound conclusions as to the motion of the solar system in space, Haydn is establishing his musical Cosmos in and about C minor [Musical example: No. 1, bars 2–7] – with ambiguities and boldnesses which show that he is fully aware of the paradox inherent in any thinkable notion of Chaos. You may think that Cosmos has already evolved to a prosaic order of tonality when Haydn's third and fourth bars can clearly assert so commonplace a phenomenon as the dominant. But four bars will no more make a Chaos than they will make a Cosmos; and you will get a much more vividly chaotic impression from statements arousing expectations which are contradicted than from statements which arouse no expectations at all. . . .

. . . Cuts inside a number are wholly Philistine, and nowhere more so than when they consist in skipping repetitions. . . . Besides the elimination of the terzet [No. 27], with its redundant introductory exposition of the chorus [No. 26], my only other cut in *The Creation* is the drastic one of ending with the greatest design Haydn ever executed, and the sublimest number since the Representation of Chaos, the duet of Adam and Eve with chorus of angels, No. 30. Everything after that is not only an anticlimax but involves the intrusion of the loss of Paradise [No. 33]. It is unfortunately possible that Haydn might be shocked at the idea of ending without another Palladian-Handelian double fugue; he probably thought that such move-ments were intrinsically grander than those of the symphonic order in which he was supreme. But I prefer to imagine that he would, after some doubts, be glad to have due recognition of his real supremacy and would come to see that another Palladian double fugue in B flat, however grand, could add nothing but anticlimax to the symphonic and choral finality of the great Adagio and Allegretto which merge the praises of Adam and Eve in those of the Heavenly Hosts and establish the key of C major as the inevitable outcome of the C minor round which the first Chaos gravitated. Thus ended, the work is considerably shorter than Bach's B minor Mass, and it falls into two parts; the two numbers [29, 30] from Haydn's Third Part being only a few minutes longer than the two movements [26, 27] excised from his Second Part. The change from the B flat of [No. 28] to the indefinitely remote E major of the representation of Morning [No. 29] is a bold step to take without interposing an interval. But it is a Haydnesque step, and it differs from precisely the same juxtaposition (D flat to G major) in the middle of Beethoven's Quartet in B flat, Op. 130, only in the Haydnesque particular that it remains a paradox whereas Beethoven's audacities of tonality are always rationalized. . . .

[No. 8]

I am told by one of the truest of Haydn-lovers that this aria does not stand the strain of 7,459 consecutive performances at Competition Festivals. Never having tried any such experiment, I am defenceless in still finding it as beautiful as anything else in Haydn, Schubert, Brahms, or any other master of lyric melody....

[No. 13]

Of the main theme, [the rising scale in bars 8–10] becomes that of the fugal climax, while [the first five notes] become the starting-point of the danger-ously simple passages for the trio of archangels. The danger of these pas-sages lies in what I believe to be Haydn's discovery of the charm of simple cadential chords held with indefinite pauses by solo voices.... The climax of the coda in the first movement of Beethoven's Second Symphony does not suffer from comparison with the end of 'The Heavens are telling', because Beethoven no more misses Haydn's point than Virgil misses the point when he translates Homer.... Quite a long book might be written about the influence of Haydn's *Creation* on later music. The innocent solo-trio pauses have been a danger to later musicians and critics because nothing is easier than to live on the income of their natural effect. The prig who is proud of his artistic conscience is in the long run (which, however, the poor fellow never gets) less detestable than the more fashionable prig who is proud of having none. It is mere snobbishness to say that Haydn's juicy vocal pauses are mere Sullivan; the difference between Haydn and Sullivan is that Haydn's self-indulgence in this matter is a small and severely disciplined element of relaxation in some of the hardest work ever achieved by mortal man – whereas Sullivan – [Music Example] *il resto nol dico*.

Karl Geiringer (1963)

From his *Haydn: A Creative Life in Music*, 2nd edn (New York, 1963), pp. 381–8. This is a revised version of a similar passage in the 1st edition of 1946, and is reprinted here by permission of W. W. Norton & Company.

It is no longer necessary to apologize for Haydn's last two oratorios. Never-theless, they do not enjoy in the English-speaking countries the position they deserve. Performances of *The Creation* are still relatively infrequent ... The great popularity that these oratorios enjoy in Austria and Germany is not paralleled in England and America, though in several respects the two works are more English than German....

Not only van Swieten's text, but also Haydn's music breathes the spirit of Handel. Haydn certainly did not copy the older master, but he found in the works of his great model an excuse for his tendency to abandon formulas accepted in his country. In Haydn's oratorio, chorus and soloists are sometimes used together, at other times alternate quickly; the form of the arias changes from number to number, but is always dependent on the text; the recitatives often assume the form of charmingly accompanied ariosos, displaying in their tone-paintings the composer's deep love of nature. All this is typical of Haydn's last period of composition, but it is doubtful that he would have dared to follow his instinct so completely, had it not been for the encouragement provided by Handel's oratorios. . . .

Better than any personal document, *The Creation* testifies to the breadth of Haydn's inner world. In this work, childlike naïveté, joy in the world of the senses, and gentle humor are combined with profound faith, nobility of expression, and hymnlike fervor. The diversity inherent in this spiritual landscape may account for the strong echo that the work, since its first performance, has evoked in the hearts of listeners.

Charles Rosen (1972)

From his *The Classical Style: Haydn, Mozart, Beethoven* (New York, 1972), pp. 370–3. Reprinted by permission of W. W. Norton & Company.

The famous depiction of chaos at the opening of the *Creation* is in 'slow-movement sonata form': nothing could show better how, for Haydn, the 'sonata' is not a form at all, but an integral part of the musical language, and even a necessary minimum for any large statement that can be made within that language. The themes are here reduced to very small fragments, as are the musical paragraphs, but the proportions of a sonata movement without an isolated development section but with articulated exposition and symmetrical recapitulation (both with two regular groups of themes) is as present as ever in Haydn's slow movements. The opening theme [Music Example: bars 1–4] is as much dynamic marking as a series of pitches, and it is later enriched by a staccato arpeggio as the movement becomes more complex. The second theme, in the relative major [bars 28–9] (actually an inversion of an earlier phrase) has an even more characteristic outline. The beginning of the recapitulation could not be more easily identifiable [40–2], and the most unusual formal device is only that the second theme is recapitulated and resolved at the tonic with the first theme in counterpoint [50–52], where the clarinet's ascending motif is a decorative form of the opening notes in the first violins quoted above [3–4].

By what, then, is chaos represented, and how can Haydn's musical language express this and still remain language? Simply by the absence of clear articulation in the large phrase-groups, which merge and blend with each other, and by the withholding of clear and definite cadences. The progression of the relative major is at first as clear as in any sonata movement in a minor tonality, but there is a sudden evasion to a surprisingly remote VIIb [16–21]; and the return to the more normal E flat major, while effected almost immediately, is never granted an ending in root position [25–8], so that the second theme begins without the firmness of the usual cadence. The extremely slow tempo, the syncopated string chords and the irregular phrase-lengths do the rest: in spite of the breadth of feeling, the facture is concentrated on movement in the miniature, and everything depends on detail.

With the two oratorio texts, the pastoral tradition at last allowed Haydn a structure which enabled him to sum up his technique and his life's work: they were to him what the *Art of Fugue* was to Bach, and the *Diabelli* Variations to Beethoven. The *Seasons* and the *Creation* are descriptions of the entire universe as Haydn knew it. The imposed simplicity of the pastoral style was the condition which made it possible to grasp subjects of such immensity: without the pretense of naïveté in the deepest sense of the spontaneous and unaffected response of the child's eye to the world, these works could not exist at all. The subject of pastoral is not Nature itself, but man's relation to nature and to what is 'natural': this is the reason for the extreme stylization of Haydn's descriptive writing in the oratorios. He did not like the purely programmatic part of his texts, and called them 'French trash', but they were an essential part of the tradition, which had, indeed, become largely French during the eighteenth century.

Appendix 1

Performance practice

In a recent book, A. Peter Brown has provided a wealth of information, drawn from primary sources, about the early performances of Haydn's *The Creation* that were directed or otherwise approved by the composer.[1] I have added further suggestions, making use of sources beyond those that were closely connected with Haydn himself.[2] This appendix is intended to provide a brief summary of the main points on which doubt may arise.

I am very far from taking the position that modern performances ought to be strictly governed by the practices of the past, still less that they should be modelled on some specific early performance. But few today will doubt that awareness of contemporary practices, as well as knowledge of the composer's intentions, is an indispensable guide to the modern performer or conductor of a historical work.

Venue

All early performances, without exception, took place in theatres, concert halls, or private salons. There was never any doubt that *The Creation* was a concert work. Performances in church were prohibited in Austria; they seem to have originated in English provincial festivals: e.g. when Part One was given at York Minster in 1823.

Language

In Haydn's time it was taken for granted that vocal works would be sung in the language of the audience. The only exceptions were Latin, the universal language of Roman Catholic church music, and Italian, which enjoyed a kind of supranational prestige in opera and in certain other vocal genres of high status. For example, *The Magic Flute*, when first performed in London in 1811, was sung in Italian translation; and *The Creation* itself was translated into Italian for several performances in Vienna during Haydn's lifetime, including the famous occasion at the University on 27 March 1808.[3]

The responsibility for translating the texts of vocal works to suit local conditions, and adapting the translation to the music, normally fell on the manager of the theatre or concert concerned, unless someone else had performed the task for him. For instance Handel's (English) oratorios were translated into German for performance by the Tonkünstler-Societät from 1779 onwards, probably by Gottfried van Swieten.

The unusual circumstance with regard to *The Creation* is that Haydn made himself responsible for the English version of the text, though delegating the task of adaptation chiefly to Swieten. His motive was not to ensure that the English language would be used in England – that could be taken for granted; it was to determine what English text would be used. Thus the English text is authentic. It is certainly appropriate to use it where English is the prevailing language of the audience. But it cannot be used without modification.

Vocal soloists

The score has parts for five characters (SSTBB), and for four unnamed soloists (SATB) in the last movement. Haydn's performances invariably announced only three soloists: the soprano sang Eve as well as Gabriel, the bass sang Adam as well as Raphael, and the tenor sang Uriel. The plan of the work clearly lends itself to this arrangement, since, when Adam and Eve arrive, Gabriel and Raphael disappear, leaving Uriel to sing the narrative. In No. 34 the brief alto solo must have been sung by someone in the chorus; this may have been true of the other solo parts in that movement also, although the fact that they have more conspicuous music than the alto suggests that these parts were taken by the three principals.

In early London performances the practice was different. Salomon announced six soloists (SSTTBB) and thus presumably used different singers for each of the five characters; the second tenor is hard to account for. Ashley's advertisements name a female soprano, a boy, three other unidentified women, two tenors, and two basses.

There are two points where the first edition shows that one of the soloists was expected to sing with the chorus: this is not always reflected in modern editions. In No. 2 Uriel is silent from bar 78 to bar 112, but sings with the chorus tenors from 121 to the end. In No. 4 Gabriel sings with the chorus sopranos whenever (s)he has no independent part. In No. 34 it is not specified that the soloists join the chorus at bar 68, but it seems highly probable. Elsewhere, soloists sang with the chorus unless they had their own parts, as is shown by solo-tutti markings in early chorus parts.[4]

Choral forces

There was considerable variation in the size of the chorus, both in performances of *The Creation* and in general practice of the time. Widely varying figures from different times and places have been collected.[5] In discussing Haydn's own performances Brown distinguishes between two types: 'chamber' renditions in private salons and more ambitious presentations, usually in public halls. In both cases, he cites the authority of Otto Biba[6] for concluding that the normal ratio of singers to instrumentalists would have been about 1:2. The 'chamber' forces may have fallen as low as eight singers on one occasion at Eisenstadt in 1800.[7] For the larger public performances 60–70 singers seems to have been the norm, out of a total of some 200 performers. 'Monster' performances began in Vienna only after Haydn's death, with the founding of the Gesellschaft der Musikfreunde in 1813.

Although Handel's oratorios had been taking on monster proportions in England since 1784 at least, *The Creation* does not appear to have shared this privilege until it entered the repertoire of the larger provincial festivals, such as the one at York in 1823. The early London performances were held at the Oratorio Concerts at Covent Garden and the King's Theatre; at the first performance, parts were copied for 120 performers. In England the general tendency was for the chorus to be about equal to the orchestra in numbers, or slightly larger. So there may have been about 60 in the chorus. Paris at this time went in for monster productions: one 1800 performance of *The Creation* had a chorus of 150 and an orchestra of 159.[8]

Viennese choruses seem to have favoured boys' voices for alto as well as soprano parts, and Brown has found no documentation of women's voices (apart from the soloists) until after the founding of the Gesellschaft der Musikfreunde. Little is known about the proportions among the different parts in Viennese choirs.[9] In England the proportions were not very consistent: the Ancient Concerts had voices (from soprano to bass) in the approximate ratio 2:1:1:1, but others were closer to 2:1:2:2. It was normal to use a preponderance of women on the soprano line, with perhaps some boys, but the alto line consisted chiefly of countertenors.

Orchestral forces

To a certain extent, the exact instrumentation of a piece of music was still, in the late eighteenth century, allowed to fluctuate according to the circumstances of a particular occasion. Both Haydn and Mozart had been known to add or substitute wind instruments in their symphonies. For large-scale events, additional players might be added to the winds and brass as well as the strings, and parts added for extra instruments, with or without the composer's sanction. A familiar example is Mozart's addition of wind parts to Handel's oratorios for the Tonkünstler-Societät.

As with the size of the chorus, Brown finds that Haydn adopted two distinct practices, one for small private occasions and the other for large-scale public use. In some cases he had only 24–30 instruments, which would hardly allow for more than half a dozen violins and one to a part everywhere else, unless some of the brass parts were left out altogether. For the large-scale events, however, the orchestra may well have been some 120 strong. This agrees quite well with the Tonkünstler parts, as described by Brown, which allow for the following conjectural numbers in each section[10]:

WOODWINDS	3 parts for 2 flutes[11]	6 players		
	3 parts for 2 oboes	6		
	3 parts for 2 clarinets	6		
	3 parts for 2 bassoons	6		
	1 contrabassoon part	1	Total	25
BRASS	3 parts for 2 horns	6 players		
	2 parts for 2 trumpets	4		
	2 parts for 2 trombones	4		
	1 bass trombone part	1	Total	15
PERCUSSION	2 timpani parts			2
STRINGS	9 first violin parts	18 players		
	9 second violin parts	18		
	6 viola parts	12		
	11 cello and bass parts	22	Total	70
KEYBOARD CONTINUO				1
			Grand total	113

These instruments did not all play all the time, though the strings may have done so. In the wind, brass and percussion parts 'solo' and 'tutti' passages were clearly marked; no doubt the 'solo' passages were played only by the front desk of each section (called 'Erste Harmonie' in the manuscript parts). These passages have been listed by Brown.[12] Moreover, additional entries for the contrabassoon and bass trombone were provided for these large-scale perform-ances.[13]

These arrangements were not used, as far as is known, in the early London performances. It is quite probable that the brass and woodwind parts were doubled, since orchestras tended to be enlarged when playing with a chorus. If, as is probable, the total orchestral forces at Salomon's and Ashley's disposal were about 55, doubled wind and brass leave about 27 for the strings. This agrees quite well with the known numbers for Salomon's subscription concerts of the 1790s: 12–15 violins, 4 violas, 3 cellos, 4 double basses.

Continuo realization

Contrary to general belief, the keyboard continuo was not obsolete in 1800. There was always a piano in the orchestra, usually at front centre stage, and its purpose was no doubt chiefly to hold the performers together and steady the tempo, in a period when there were few rehearsals. Many surviving scores have bass figures added in manuscript, attesting to the survival of continuo practice.

In *The Creation*, a piano was of course required for the secco recitatives. But there is incontestable evidence that Haydn expected it to play in the orchestrated portions as well.[14] First, there are two passages which he marked 'senza cembalo' (the rising of the moon, No. 12, bars 26–36; and the Trio, No. 27, where the string basses enter at bar 34). Second, two manuscript full scores associated with Haydn have partially figured basses added in a later hand, presumably that of the continuo player.[15] It is clear from these added figures that the pianist played from the double bass part rather than the cello part where the two separated; it was, in fact, the old *Generalbass*.

It must be assumed, then, that the piano plays with the orchestra everywhere, though its presence may be difficult to detect in the total sound. There are two places where it has an essential role: No. 3, bar 32, where Haydn in the midst of an accompanied recitative leaves one bass note unharmonized; and No. 18, bars 124–7, where the trio of soloists is accompanied by the bass alone. As there is no 'senza cembalo' marking in either passage we must assume that Haydn intended these basses to be realized.

English performances also included a piano continuo player – indeed, they may still have done so after the practice had dropped out on the Continent.[16] Sir George Smart (1776–1867) continued to 'preside at the pianoforte' over the concerts he conducted throughout most of his long career. The score he used, probably from 1813 onwards, has Clementi's realizations of the secco recitatives pasted in, and has a manuscript C-major chord marked 'Piano forte' added under the word 'And' at bar 89 of No. 1.

The secco recitatives were accompanied by one or two cellos and a double bass as well as the piano, as is shown by the early string parts. Two contemporary realizations are available in published vocal scores: those by Sigismund Neukomm (Vienna, [1800]) and Clementi (London, [1800]). Clementi's has full chords in the left hand as well as the right, and indicates arpeggiation for some chords but not others.[17] Neukomm's version is more sparing.

Later in the nineteenth century, when the piano was no longer used in the orchestra, it became usual to accompany even the secco recitatives with cello and bass alone. The Tonkünstler parts were emended in such a way that a group of cellos provided the realization of the chords.[18] In England it became the custom for Robert Lindley and Domenico Dragonetti to accompany the recitatives on a solo cello and double bass: Lindley apparently improvised realizations on his cello.[19] In Peters' edition of *c.* 1872 the secco recitatives are scored up for full four-part strings.

Tempo

Brown points out that 'Haydn's preferences for tempos were overall on the fast side',[20] and cites some contemporary evidence. Unfortunately this provides us with little guidance, for it only shows that Haydn's tempos were faster than the average in his day, and we do not know what the average was.

Tempo is difficult to establish for works dating from before the metronome came into general use after about 1813. There were many living, however, who could have set down the metronomic tempos for *The Creation* from their memories of Haydn's practice. According to a contemporary account, Antonio Salieri did precisely this when he acquired a Maelzel metronome in about 1813,[21] but only four of his tempos were reported, and they were disputed by contemporaries.

There is, however, a valuable set of metronome tempos from Sigismund Neukomm, a pupil of Haydn's who was undoubtedly present at many early performances and who prepared a vocal score of *The Creation* published by Artaria at Vienna in 1800. In the preface to his revised vocal score of 1832 he wrote:

Having so often heard this work performed under the direction of its author, and having also, on many occasions, conducted it myself in his presence, I am enabled, I hope, to render a real service to the musical world by fixing (by the metronome) the movement of all the pieces; several of which have hitherto been performed in a time never intended by the composer.

These tempos have been described in full elsewhere.[22] They suggest that Haydn did, indeed, take most movements faster than they are generally taken today. One of the few exceptions is No. 1, which Neukomm marked ♪ 108, both at the beginning and again at the entry of the chorus.

In No. 6, at bar 73, where Haydn gave no new tempo mark, Neukomm wrote in his score: 'N.B. Always the same movement to the End, and NOT slower.' Evidently this was to correct a tendency to dawdle in this last section of the aria – a tendency which is noticeable also in several modern recordings. He also wrote 'In time' after the pause in No. 13, at bar 92. We may conclude from Neukomm's evidence that Haydn generally preferred to keep quite strictly to tempo.

Embellishment

It was, of course, customary for solo singers to embellish their arias, especially at fermatas and in da capo repeats. But the practice of Italian opera should not be transferred wholesale to this work. Embellishment would no doubt have tended to be less in oratorio than in opera, less in German or English than in Italian; there are no strict da capo arias here, although No. 8 approaches this category; and, according to Brown, Haydn himself was conservative in this matter.[23]

One early set of parts shows cadenza-like embellishments at fermatas in two accompanied recitatives: Nos. 29 and 31.[24]

Fortunately, an unusually complete set of written-out embellishments approved, or at least tolerated, by Haydn has come down in some of the early performing materials. These have been thoroughly discussed and in many cases transcribed by Brown.[25]

Standard ornaments

The more standard types of ornament – the trill, turn and appoggiatura (short and long) – appear from time to time in this work. They do not raise unusual problems. The general rules for their interpretation work well in practice here.

In Italian recitatives, phrase endings on a repeated note are subject to modification by a well-understood convention: the first of the two written notes is raised by one step, or, where there is a drop of a fourth or more from the note before, by that larger interval. This convention can be readily applied to similar feminine endings, of two or three syllables, in the German or English versions of *The Creation*.

There are, however, many masculine phrase endings of a type that has few parallels in Italian recitative. In Ex. 14, for instance, Haydn specified the characteristic 'Italianate' endings for the German 'gut war' and 'Finsternis' and for the English 'darkness', all feminine; but he (or Swieten) left plain the masculine endings 'Licht', 'light' and 'good'. In some performances singers add slurred appoggiaturas to these masculine endings: for instance, they might sing the two notes allotted to 'gut war' to the English word 'good' in bar 92.

Whether there is historical justification for this practice is a question which could be answered only by a wide-ranging study. In so far as can be judged from Haydn's score itself, it seems that Haydn wrote in appoggiaturas for the German text when he wanted them;[26] Swieten, with or without Haydn's direct supervision, let them stand with the English text, and added one more on the word 'earth' (No. 5, bar 8). It seems a sound inference that one should not add appoggiaturas to masculine endings where none are marked.

Example 14 No. 1, bars 89–95, German and English forms

Dynamics and articulation

Haydn's dynamic markings are generally explicit, while still leaving some room for discretion. As was customary, he wrote no dynamics in the solo singers' parts: presumably they were free to vary their expression at will. When the accompaniment changes from *forte* to *piano*, the reason may be, in some cases, to ensure that the voice is not overpowered. Elsewhere, however, it has to be taken as a hint that the voice, too, should moderate its tone: two clear examples are at the words 'Softly purling' in No. 6, bar 75, and 'Her softly smiling virgin looks' in No. 24, bar 65.

The only unequivocal marks of articulation in Haydn's score are the staccato markings, either dots or wedges, found here and there in the instrumental parts, and even in the chorus parts for the concluding amens. The slur is notoriously difficult to interpret in this period. The only thing one can say with certainty is that notes connected by a slur are to be performed *legato*: in vocal parts this means a melisma (two or more notes to a syllable); in wind and string parts it discourages breathing or change of bow. What is far less certain, however, is that the end of a slur indicates detachment of the last note from what follows,[27] or that successive slurs over a melodic line in string parts show where the bow is to be changed. This is what Brown assumes when he refers to the slurs in string parts as 'bowings', and reports on the bewildering diversity of slur placement among the early sources.[28]

The simple explanation for this diversity is that series of slurs over a continuous melodic passage indicated only *legato*; the breaks between the slurs had little significance, and it was left to each player to decide where to change the bow. It is for this reason that whenever a sparingly edited, scholarly edition of classical orchestral music is performed today, the conductor or his deputy finds it necessary to mark bowings in all the string parts to produce uniformity of bowing in each section. Such uniformity has been considered important since the rise of disciplined rehearsing and conducting in the mid-nineteenth century. But there is little reason to think that it mattered to Haydn or his contemporaries.

Appendix 2

Editions currently available and numbering of movements

Editions in Print

The principal editions now available are arranged chronologically below, according to the date of their earliest publication. Pirated reprints are not listed.

A. Borough Green: Novello. English text only. Vocal score, ed. Vincent Novello, 1847 (revised 1858 and *c.* 1900); full score on hire, 1859.

B. Leipzig, London and New York: C. F. Peters. German and English texts. Vocal score, *c.* 1860 (revised *c.* 1891 and 1932); full score on hire, *c.* 1872.

C. Leipzig and Wiesbaden: Breitkopf & Härtel. German, English and French texts. Vocal score, ed. Paul Klengel, *c.* 1885; full score on hire, edition **G**.

D. Paris: Choudens. French text only. Vocal score, *c.* 1890. Full score on hire (not seen).

E. New York: G. Schirmer. English text only. Similar to edition **A**. Vocal score, *c.* 1890; full score on hire, a reprint of edition **G**.

F. Leipzig, London and Zurich: Ernst Eulenburg. German text only. Miniature full score, 1907 (reprinted from an earlier Peters edition).

G. Leipzig: Breitkopf & Härtel (Joseph Haydns Werke, Serie 16, Band V). German text only. Full score, ed. Eusebius Mandyczewski, 1924.

H. New York: Lawson-Gould. English text only. Vocal score, 1957. A photographic reprint of edition **B** with, superimposed, a new English version by Robert Shaw and Alice Parker.

I. London: Peters Edition. English text only. Vocal score, ed. Nicholas Temperley, 1988. Full score on hire, based on edition **B** with revisions.

J. Oxford: Oxford University Press. German and English texts. Vocal score, ed. A. Peter Brown, 1990; full score forthcoming.

Numbering of movements

Neither Haydn's edition nor any of the early librettos numbered the movements of *The Creation*. The table below shows how they are numbered in the principal modern editions and secondary sources. The first column gives the numberings followed in this book. Orchestrally scored movements are listed in boldface type.

Editions	B D F H I	C D G J	A E	
Secondary sources	Landon Temperley	Brown		Hoboken
PART ONE				
Introduction (Representation of Chaos)	⎫ 1	⎧ 1	1	1a
Recitative (Raphael, Uriel) and **Chorus**	⎭	⎨ 2	2	1b,c
Aria (Uriel) and **Chorus**, 'Nun schwanden'/ 'Now vanish'	2	3	3	2
Recitative (Raphael)	3	4	4	3
Solo (Gabriel) and **Chorus**, 'Mit Staunen'/'The marv'lous work'	4	5	5	4
Recitative (Raphael)	5	6	6	5a
Aria (Raphael), 'Rollend'/'Rolling'	6	7	7	5b
Recitative (Gabriel)	7	8	8	6a
Aria (Gabriel), 'Nun beut die Flur'/'With verdure clad'	8	9	9	6b
Recitative (Uriel)	9	10	10	7a
Chorus, 'Stimmt an die Saiten'/'Awake the harp'	10	11	11	7b,c
Recitative (Uriel)	11	12	12	8a
Recitative (Uriel)	12	13	13	8b
Chorus with Soli, 'Die Himmel erzählen'/ 'The heavens are telling'	13	14	14	8c
PART TWO				
Recitative (Gabriel)	14	15	15	9a
Aria (Gabriel), 'Auf starkem Fittige'/'On mighty pens'	15	16	16	9b
Recitative (Raphael)	16	17	17	10
Recitative (Raphael)	17	18	18	11a
Trio, 'In holder Anmut'/'Most beautiful appear'	18 ⎫	⎫ 19 ⎧	19 ⎫	⎫ 11b
Trio and **Chorus**, 'Der Herr ist gross'/'The Lord is great'	19 ⎭	⎭ ⎨	20 ⎭	⎭
Recitative (Raphael)	20	20	21	12a
Recitative (Raphael)	21	21	22	12b
Aria (Raphael), 'Nun scheint'/'Now heav'n'	22	22	23	12c

Editions	**B D F** **H I**	**C D** **G J**	**A** **E**	
Secondary sources	Landon Temperley	Brown		Hoboken
Recitative (Uriel)	23	23	24	13a
Aria (Uriel), 'Mit Würd' und Hoheit'/'In native worth'	24	24	25	13b
Recitative (Raphael)	25	25	26	14a
Chorus, 'Vollendet'/'Achieved'	26		27	14b
Trio, 'Zu dir'/'On thee'	27	26	27A	14c
Chorus, 'Vollendet'/'Achieved'	28		27B	14b,d
PART THREE				
Recitative (Uriel)	29	27	28	15a
Hymn, 'Von deiner Güt''/'By thee with bliss'	30	28	29	15b,c,d
Recitative (Adam, Eve)	31	29	30	16a
Duet, 'Holde Gattin'/'Graceful consort'	32	30	31	16b,c
Recitative (Uriel)	33	31	32	17a
Chorus, 'Singt dem Herren'/'Sing the Lord'	34	32	33	17b

Notes

Works for which full details are given in the Bibliography (pp. 131–3) are cited by author and short title in these notes.

1 Background

1 Smither, *Oratorio*, pp. 35–6.
2 *Ibid.*, pp. 51–62.
3 *Ibid.*, pp. 361–76.
4 *Ibid.*, p. 344.
5 Dean, *Handel's Dramatic Oratorios, passim*, especially chapter 3.
6 William Hayes, *The Art of Composing Music by a Method Entirely New* (London, 1751). Dean (*Handel's Dramatic Oratorios*, p. 105) dismisses this statement as 'of course ironical', but such an interpretation seems far-fetched. Rollo H. Myers (*Handel's Messiah*, pp. 150–1) gives further support from Charles Burney, whom he quotes as saying that Handel 'was always aspiring at numbers in his scores and his orchestra', but I have been unable to trace this reference to its source.
7 Myers, *Handel's Messiah*, pp. 215–20. For the national and political significance of the 1784 festival see Weber, 'Handel Commemoration'.
8 Landon, *Haydn*, vol. III, pp. 83–4.
9 Giuseppe Carpani, *Le Haydine* (Milan, 1812), pp. 162–3; trans. Landon, vol. III, p. 84.
10 Geiringer, *Haydn*, p. 381.
11 Smither, *Oratorio*, p. 161.
12 *Ibid.*, pp. 168–78.
13 *K. k. privilegierte Realzeitung* 14 (1775), 219; trans. Landon, vol. II, p. 215.
14 Drury, 'Haydn's *Seven Last Words*', pp. 6–12. Drury offers the fullest account of *The Seven Last Words* in all its ramifications, and is the basis for the details given here.
15 Landon, *Haydn*, vol. V, pp. 93, 182, 199. Only a selection of movements was performed at the London oratorios, on 16 March 1803 (repeated 18 March).
16 See, for instance, Rosen, *Classical Style*, p. 370. Rushton (*Classical Music*, p. 129) places it on at least as high a level as *The Creation*.
17 Blume, *Classic and Romantic Music*, p. 73. In fact, as we have seen, the reception of *The Seasons* was by no means immediate or universal.

2 Theology

1 Stromberg, *Religious Liberalism*, p. 21.
2 Numbering of movements follows the Peters and Eulenburg editions (see below, pp. 119–20). Bar numbers follow Peters, since Eulenburg's bar numbering is erratic.

3 See Nicholas Temperley, *The Music of the English Parish Church* (Cambridge, 1979), vol. I, p. 232 and vol. II, pp. 138–45.
4 Smith, 'Intellectual Contexts', p. 126.
5 Thomas Chubb, *Posthumous Works* (London, 1748), vol. I, p. 157.
6 David Hume, *The Natural History of Religion* (London, 1757).
7 Stromberg, *Religious Liberalism*, p. 59.
8 *Ibid.*, p. 110.
9 Smith, 'Intellectual Contexts', p. 120.
10 Nettl, *Mozart and Masonry*, p. 4.
11 Milton, *Paradise Lost*, VII: 505–16. (*Front*: face; *magnanimous*: high-minded).
12 *Ibid.*, IV: 650–6.
13 Stern, 'Haydn's "Schöpfung"', pp. 121–98.
14 *Ibid.*, pp. 158, 160.
15 *Ibid.*, pp. 162–8.
16 *Ibid.*, pp. 169–71.
17 Pauly, 'Reforms', pp. 373–4.
18 Landon, *Haydn*, vol. IV, p. 346.
19 For a summary see Landon, vol. IV, pp. 349–50.
20 Nettl, *Mozart and Masonry*, p. 16.
21 Griesinger, *Biographische Notizen*, pp. 53–5; trans. Gottwals, *Haydn*, pp. 53–4.
22 Haydn to Jean Philipp Krüger, 22 September 1802, cited Stern, '"Schöpfung"', p. 192.
23 These are transcribed in Walter, 'Textbücher', and are translated with commentary in Landon, vol. IV, pp. 350–2.
24 Levarie, 'Closing Numbers'.

3 The Libretto

1 *AMZ* 1 (1798–9), cols. 254–5; trans. Olleson, 'Origin and Libretto', pp. 149–50.
2 Griesinger, *Biographische Notizen*, p. 37; Dies, *Biographische Nachrichten*, p. 158; trans. Gottwals, *Haydn*, pp. 37, 174. Cf. Olleson, 'Origin and Libretto', pp. 150–1.
3 Stern ('"Schöpfung"') treats the text as if it were a product of trends in German literature and philosophy.
4 *The Times*, 27 March 1800. The French title, too, was *La création du monde*.
5 Temperley, 'New Light'.
6 The letter (in French) is transcribed in Pohl, *Haydn in London*, vol. III, pp. 130–1.
7 Compare the structure of the completed oratorio as shown below, p. 48, Table 1.
8 Milton, *Paradise Lost* IV: 252–60, 557–61.
9 *AMZ* 4 (1801–2), cols. 385–96. See pp. 89–92 below.
10 For details see Temperley, 'New Light', p. 202.
11 Budapest, National Library, Ha.I.12; partly transcribed Walter, 'Textbücher', pp. 249–57.
12 *Paradise Lost* V: 153–208, IV: 411–775. For the title 'Hymn' see below, p. 86.
13 An abridged text of this document, with critical commentary, appears in Walter, 'Textbücher'; a commentary on the annotations is in Landon, *Haydn*, vol. IV, pp. 351–2.
14 Mörner, 'Haydniana', pp. 24ff.
15 This epithet may not have sounded eccentric to Georgian ears; the *Oxford English Dictionary* quotes a line from John Arbuthnot's *Essay Concerning the Nature of Aliments* (1731), II, 40: 'An Animal, in order to be moveable, must be flexible'.
16 *Paradise Lost*, VII: 399–403.
17 Howard Smither, whose *History of the Oratorio* is by far the most authoritative work on the subject, recognizes two types of German oratorios in this period – 'dramatic' and 'lyric' – and defines the English oratorio as 'usually dramatic', though the Latin and Italian genres

were normally dramatic and differed only in subject matter from *opera seria* (Smither, *Oratorio*, vol. III, pp. 4–6, 201, 331–40).

18 Olleson, 'Origin and Libretto'; Temperley, 'New Light'.

19 This was established by Paula Baumgärtner in her dissertation 'Gottfried van Swieten'; its significance was pointed out by Olleson, 'Origin and Libretto', p. 156.

20 Full details of all such variants are tabulated in Temperley, 'New Light', pp. 201–3.

21 K. Goedeke, ed., *Schillers Briefwechsel mit Ch. G. Körner*, 2nd edn (Leipzig, 1878), vol. II, p. 363; trans. Landon, *Haydn*, vol. IV, p. 343. By 1802 these criticisms were beginning to have their effect even in Vienna: see Landon, *Haydn*, vol. V, p. 236, and p. 89 below.

22 Max Friedländer, 'Van Swieten', cited Landon, *Haydn*, vol. IV, p. 344; Stern, "Schöpfung", p. 129.

23 This page is reproduced in Temperley, 'New Light', p. 195, plate 1.

24 *RISM* H-2523.

4 Composition, performance and reception

1 Charles H. Purday in *The Leisure Hour* (London, 1880), p. 528. Cited Olleson, 'Origin and Libretto', p. 152.

2 *AMZ* 1 (1798–9), cols. 254–5. Trans. Olleson, 'Origin and Libretto', p. 150.

3 *Musica Divina* 9 (1921), 10. Trans. Landon, *Haydn*, vol. IV, p. 115.

4 Landon, *Haydn*, vol. IV, pp. 351–2.

5 Franz Grillparzer, *Werke* XV/4 (Stuttgart, 1893), 124. Trans. Landon, *Haydn*, vol. IV, p. 353. Grillparzer's source was 'a well-informed contemporary' who himself took part in these pre-rehearsals.

6 Mörner, 'Haydniana', pp. 24–8; trans. Landon, *Haydn*, vol. IV, pp. 251, 256, 264.

7 See below, p. 70, Ex.6. For detailed discussion see Temperley, 'New Light', pp. 204–11.

8 Landon, *Haydn*, vol. III, p. 353.

9 *Ibid.*, pp. 352–88. Further analysis was undertaken in a paper by A. Peter Brown at the Royal Musical Association conference in April 1989.

10 GB:Lbl, Add.MS.28613, f.2v; transcribed Landon, *Haydn*, vol. IV, p. 374.

11 A:Wn, Codex 16835, f. XVr.; cited Geiringer, 'Haydn's Sketches', p. 304.

12 The whole process is set out with full musical illustration in Brown, *Performing*, pp. 40–41.

13 A:Wn, Codex 16835, f.XVIIv.; transcribed Landon. *Haydn*, vol. IV, p. 378.

14 *Haydn*, vol. IV, pp. 384–5, from A:Wn, Codex 16835, f.Ir. See also Geiringer, 'Haydn's Sketches', pp. 302–4.

15 US:NYp, from the collection of Anton Schmid and Alexandr Posonyi. Facsimile in Emanuel Winternitz, *Musical Autographs* (Princeton, 1955), Plate 57; transcribed Landon, *Haydn*, vol. IV, p. 357.

16 See Landon, *Haydn*, vol. IV, pp. 358–73.

17 For a thorough discussion of the manuscript sources see Brown, *Performing*, chap. 1.

18 Mörner, 'Haydniana', p. 28; trans, Landon, *Haydn*, vol. IV, p. 318.

19 Landon, *Haydn*, vol. IV, pp. 320–2.

20 Griesinger, *Biographische Notizen*, p. 37; trans. Gottwals, *Haydn*, p. 38.

21 *AMZ* 1 (1798–9), cols. 333–4.

22 Not, as Landon states (before quoting the text in full), a 'request for the audience not to applaud between numbers'.

23 Brown, *Performing*, pp. 20–1.

24 See p. 112 below.

25 A number of contemporary accounts are quoted by Landon, *Haydn*, vol. IV, pp. 453–8.

26 Landon, *Haydn*, vol. V, p. 361.

27 See, for instance, *AMZ* (June, 1799); trans. Landon, *Haydn*, vol. IV, p. 471
28 Landon, *Haydn*, vol. IV, p. 542.
29 *Ibid.*, vol. IV, pp. 622–31.
30 See Brown, *Performing*, p. 10.
31 Berlin Mus.ms.9851. See above, p. 28.
32 *AMZ, Intelligenz Blatt XV* (June, 1799), cols. 73–4; trans. Landon, *Haydn*, vol. IV, p. 471.
33 Brown, *Performing*, chaps. 2–4 and appendixes 3–5.
34 Most of these are listed in *RISM* (A/I, nos.H2526–41), Hoboken, *Haydn* (XXI:2), or both.
35 *Trois sonates pour le pianoforte avec accompagnement d'un violon composées sur les idées prises de l'oratoire de J.Haydn: La Création et dédiées à Monsieur le Prince Auguste de Hohenlohe Ingelfingen par Joseph Woelfl.* Op.14. Leipzig: Breitkopf & Härtel, [1801].
36 From the preface to the Novello piano/vocal score of *The Creation* (London, [1842]) signed 'John Bishop, Cheltenham, Nov. 1842'. For further details see Temperley, 'New Light', pp. 191–2.
37 *The Times*, 5 April. The exchange is quoted in full by Landon, *Haydn*, vol. IV, pp. 573–6.
38 For details see p. 110 below.
39 See newspaper notices transcribed by Landon, *Haydn*, vol. IV, pp. 574–7.
40 For details see Temperley, 'New Light', p. 210, n. 43.
41 George Alexander Macfarren, preface to a libretto of *The Creation* published by the Sacred Harmonic Society in 1854 (quoted below, pp. 96–8). A copy of Haydn's published score used by Smart for many years is extant (GB:Lbl, K.10.b.22). It has pages of recitatives pasted in from Clementi's edition, and MS. chorus parts with English text based on Clementi's version; and it has two cuts marked: No. 15, bars 58–86; No. 32, bars 174–265.
42 Landon, *Haydn*, vol. IV, p. 578.
43 *AMZ* 3 (1800–01), cols. 269–70, 415, 509–13; trans. Landon, *Haydn*, vol. IV, pp. 579–81.
44 *La création du monde. Oratorio en trois parties ... traduit de l'allemand, mis en vers français par Joseph A. Ségur, arrangé pour être exécuté au Théâtre des Arts par D. Steibelt (exécuté le 3 nivose an 9e)* (Paris: Mlles Erard; Lyon: Garnier, 1801).
45 Several are cited by Landon, *Haydn*, vol. IV, pp. 578–80.
46 *AMZ* 3 (1800–01), col. 509; trans. Landon, *Haydn*, vol. IV, p. 580.
47 *AMZ* 3 (1800–01), col. 269.
48 Rufus A. Grider, *Music in Bethlehem, Pennsylvania, from 1741 to 1871* (Philadelphia, 1873), p. 6. An organ/vocal score copied in the hand of Johann Friedrich Peter and inscribed 'Coll. musicum/in Bethlm/1811' survives in the library of the Philharmonic Society of Bethlehem, as do several sets of solo and choral parts of similar date. For this information I am indebted to Richard D. Claypool, who kindly supplied me with the results of his research.
49 Charles C. Perkins and John S. Dwight, *History of the Handel and Haydn Society of Boston, Massachusetts*, vol. I (Boston, 1883–93), pp. 43, 52–3, 69.
50 H. Earle Johnson, *First Performances in America to 1900* (Detroit, 1979), p. 187.
51 Thomas Hastings, *Dissertation on Musical Taste* (New York, 1853), p. 238.
52 Brown, *Performing*, p. 21; see also Koury, *Orchestral Performance Practices*, p. 170.
53 Landon, *Haydn*, vol. V, p. 408.
54 *AMZ* 4 (1801–2), cols. 385–96; trans. Landon, *Haydn*, vol. IV, pp. 592–7. For an excerpt see pp. 89–92 below.
55 *Zeitung für die elegante Welt* 45 (14 April 1801), cited Landon, *Haydn*, vol. IV, p. 580, n. 1.
56 See, for instance, the *AMZ* review of 1802, parts of which are quoted on pp. 89–92 below.
57 *AMZ* 3 (1800–1), cols. 289–96; trans. Landon, *Haydn*, vol. IV, pp. 586–9.
58 Trans. Le Huray and Day, *Music and Aesthetics*, pp. 278–9.
59 *Ibid.*, pp. 302, 332, 440.
60 Hector Berlioz, 'L'imitation en musique', *Revue et gazette musicale de Paris* 4 (1837), p. 10; trans. Jacques Barzun, *The Pleasures of Music* (London, 1952), p. 214.

61 Berlioz, letter of 8 February 1859, in *Correspondance générale*, vol. V (Paris, 1989), p. 654; translation mine. The sets of dots in this passage are copied from the source.

62 Richard von Preger and Robert Hirschfeld, *Geschichte der k.k. Gesellschaft der Musikfreunde in Wien* (Vienna, 1912), pp. 306–19.

63 Hanslick, *Concertwesens*, vol. II, pp. 1–6; Landon, *Haydn*, vol. V, p. 422.

64 Clemens Höslinger, 'Der überwundene Standpunkt: Joseph Haydn in der Wiener Musikkritik des 19. Jahrhunderts', in *Beiträge zur Musikgeschichte des 18. Jahrhunderts: Publikationen des Instituts für Österreichische Kulturgeschichte* (Vienna, 1971), p. 141; trans. Landon, *Haydn*, vol. V, p. 424.

65 See pp. 98–9 below.

66 Schenker, 'Schöpfung'. See pp. 100–03 below.

67 See, for instance, the changes in the text of No. 33 in Samuel Webbe's edition of 1808. At the Edinburgh Festival of 1815 Nos. 31–34 were omitted (see George F. Graham, *An Account of the First Edinburgh Musical Festival* (Edinburgh, 1816). In 1834 an English critic pronounced the subject matter of Part 3 an anti-climax (see p. 95 below). For whatever reason, the omission of the concluding movements persisted in British custom into the twentieth century: it was even recommended and carried out by Tovey, though on the grounds of *musical* anticlimax and 'the intrusion of the loss of Paradise' (see p. 105 below).

68 *Monthly Magazine* (March 1811). See p. 93–4 below. This passage is inaccurately described and transcribed by Landon, *Haydn*, vol. V, p. 410.

69 Thomas Busby, *A General History of Music* (London, 1819), vol. II, pp. 399–401; cited Landon, *Haydn*, vol. V, p. 412. See pp. 94–5 below).

70 See, for instance, William Millington, *Sketches of Local Musicians and Musical Societies* (Pendlebury, 1884), *passim*.

71 See the collection of programmes, 1837–81, in the British Library, d. 493.

72 John F. Runciman, *Haydn* (London, 1908), pp. 81–2.

73 John F. Runciman, *Old Scores and New Readings* (London, 1899), p. 92; cited Landon, *Haydn*, vol. V, p. 425.

74 See, for instance, Schnorr, 'Oratorium', pp. 929–30, and Hermann Grabner, introduction to the Eulenburg miniature score, dated 'Leipzig, November 1925'. Grabner does maintain, though, that because of its craftsmanship and its wonderful simplicity Haydn's work still remains one of the most valuable jewels (*kostbarsten Schätze*) of the oratorio repertoire.

75 Tovey, 'Creation', p. 114.

76 It was primarily Tovey's opinion that prompted Siegmund Levarie to offer a defence or justification for what he called the 'commonplace conventionality of the musical substance of the second duet', as discussed above. So it is worth pointing out that Hermann Grabner, a distinguished German contemporary of Tovey's, considered the love duet superior to the Hymn (No. 30), because of its blossoming melodic line and the depth of its expression ('blühenden Melodik und Tiefe des Ausdrucks': see his introduction to the Eulenburg miniature score, 1925, p. vii).

77 Rosen, *Classical Style*, pp. 366, 369.

78 *Ibid.*, p. 370. In placing the two oratorios 'among the greatest works of the century', Rosen overlooked the fact that they were written in different centuries!

79 *Ibid.*, p. 373. See pp. 107–8 below.

80 'Beautiful world, where are you? Return, lovely golden age of nature!' From Schiller's *Die Götter Griechenlands*, set to music in Schubert's 1819 song of the same title (D 677).

5 Design of the work

1 Levarie, 'The Closing Numbers of *Die Schöpfung*', already discussed in chapter 2. Levarie's tonal analysis does not inspire confidence. He states, for example, that 'The love duet . . .

(No. 32) does not leave the tonic; the occurring accidentals serve merely to confirm the main harmonic function of E flat major' (p. 318). In fact Eve's first solo (bars 31–52) is entirely in the dominant key.

2 Smither, *Oratorio*, p. 67.

3 *Ibid.*, p. 167.

4 Drury, '*Seven Last Words*', p. 78.

5 As mentioned above (p. 33), Haydn originally planned No. 13 in D major.

6 Tovey, 'Creation', p. 142.

7 Landon, *Haydn*, vol. IV, p. 397.

8 *Ibid.*, vol. IV, p. 399; vol. V, p. 128.

9 Steblin, *Key Characteristics*, pp. 174–9, 182.

10 I am grateful to Julian Rushton for drawing my attention to this.

6 Musical analysis

1 Landon, *Haydn*, vol. IV, pp. 414–26 provides a movement-by-movement description.

2 For full discussion see Riedel-Martiny, '*Verhältnis*', pp. 209–16.

3 Smither, *Oratorio*, pp. 56, 58.

4 Dean, *Handel's Dramatic Oratorios*, p. 163.

5 Tovey, 'Creation', p. 127.

6 For example, in *Tobia* Haydn illustrated the words 'trema' and 'onda' in No. 4a, bars 16 and 25, and 'profondo orrido abisso' in No. 13a, bars 13–21. In each case the music follows or coincides with the words it depicts. Of course, in works for the stage, music often accompanies and illustrates action which is followed by a sung comment; but that is not the same thing.

7 In many editions this is wrongly marked *forte*.

8 Brown, *Performing*, p. 26.

9 Although No. 2 is headed 'Aria' in the first edition and No. 4 'Chor', they are both treated here as 'arias with chorus'. In each case, what begins as a normal aria is finally taken over by the chorus.

10 Smither, *Oratorio*, pp. 78–82, 374–5.

11 The question is discussed in depth in Smither, *Oratorio*, pp. 80–1.

12 See Jonathan Rennert, *William Crotch (1775–1847): Composer, Artist, Teacher* (Lavenham, 1975), pp. 43–4.

13 In some performances and recordings this is interpreted as a cello solo. In the first edition the part is marked 'Violoncello' while the bass line is on a stave labelled 'Bassi'; but this is the usual designation where the cellos and basses have separate staves, and early performance parts show no sign that a solo was intended here.

14 Levarie, 'Closing Numbers', p. 318. It was the tune of this Allegro that Haydn quoted in the 'Schöpfungs-messe' of 1801, and which gave it its name. Levarie goes too far, however, in equating this 2/4 conclusion solely with low characters in *opera buffa* and *Singspiel* (p. 319). It was not unusual to end a love duet for 'high' *opera seria* characters in a similar way. Haydn did so in Armida and Rinaldo's duet 'Cara, sarò fedele' in *Armida* and in Orfeo and Euridice's duet 'Come il foco' in *L'anima del filosofo*. The last has many points in common with the present movement, including most of the characteristics Levarie enumerates. To do this in an oratorio was, admittedly, uncommon: and I would agree with Levarie that it was calculated for wide popularity with parts of the Viennese public that might not respond to the normal oratorio manner.

15 Trans. Landon, *Haydn*, vol. IV, p. 351.

16 Tovey, 'Creation', p. 132.

17 John Crosse, *An Account of the Grand Musical Festival, Held in September, 1823, in the Cathedral Church of York* (York, 1825), p. 336; cited Landon, *Haydn*, vol. V, p. 411.

18 See Nicholas Temperley, *The Music of the English Parish Church* (Cambridge, 1979), vol. II, ex. 54; *The Hymnal 1982* (New York, 1985), hymn 409, tune 'Creation'.

19 This is the view of Brown, *Performing*, p. 43.

20 Frederick Corder, 'Programme-Music', in George Grove, *A Dictionary of Music and Musicians*, vol. III (London, 1883), p. 36.

21 Brown, *Performing*, p. 72.

22 Rosen, *Classical Style*, p. 370.

23 The progression from bar 8 to bar 9 struck a contemporary reviewer as 'truly new and grand': *AMZ* 3 (1800–01), col. 295; trans. Landon, *Haydn*, vol. IV, p. 588.

24 Trans. Landon, *Haydn*, vol. IV, pp. 251–2.

25 Tovey, 'Creation', pp. 142, 145.

26 A true refrain, of course, repeats the same words at each occurrence. These passages only suggest refrains by the metrical change and the fact that a chorus follows each solo.

7 Excerpts from critical essays

1 In fact, as we have seen, the original text did assign the biblical narrative to an unnamed angel and the descriptive arias to voice types only. The named angels were a subsequent addition by either Haydn or Swieten.

2 In fact No. 2, the aria being considered here, is in the present throughout in the English text, but Swieten's translation begins in the past ('schwanden ... entstand') and continues in the present ('weicht ... keimt ... erstarrt', etc.).

3 In fact the main objection expressed by the writer to No. 2, that it is [partly] in the past tense, does not apply to the other arias in their German form. In No. 3, however, which is a recitative, part secco, part accompanied, Swieten used the past tense throughout, emending the illogical change to the present tense found in the English text.

4 It is difficult to follow Gardiner's analysis at this point. It is the strings, without double basses, that play in the passage in question.

5 Actually the contrabassoon does not appear until the 'Light' (bar 86); perhaps Gardiner refers to the entry of the trombones after a descending phrase for bassoons, cellos and basses, at bar 21. It is possible, of course, that additional contrabassoon parts were used in some English performances, but there is no record of this.

6 In fact, *Tobia* had been 'enormously successful and called the attention of the Viennese to Haydn's extraordinary ability', and was followed by performances at Berlin, Rome, Lisbon and Leipzig (Smither, *Oratorio*, vol. III, pp. 163–4).

7 This probably refers to Haydn's remarks to Dies as reported in Dies, *Nachrichten*, p. 108, trans. Gottwals, *Haydn*, p. 139. 'He spoke to himself during the composing [of a piece of church music]. "I prayed to God not like a miserable sinner in despair but calmly, slowly. In this I felt that an infinite God would surely have mercy on his finite creature, pardoning dust for being dust. These thoughts cheered me up. I experienced a sure joy so confident that as I wished to express the words of the prayer, I could not suppress my joy, but gave vent to my happy spirits and wrote above the *miserere*, etc. Allegro."'

8 This is the speculative theory that the solar system originated in a large nebulous mass which later solidified to form the sun and planets. Tovey refers to Kant's *Allgemeine Naturgeschichte und Theorie des Himmels* (1755) and Laplace's *Exposition du système du monde* (Paris, 1796).

9 This statement cannot be verified. No newspaper of this name has been traced.

Appendix 1

1 Brown, *Performing*.
2 Temperley, 'Haydn's Tempos'.
3 Brown, *Performing*, Table 1, pp. 2–7.
4 *Ibid.*, p. 23.
5 Koury, *Orchestral Performance Practices*, pp. 169–70.
6 Biba, *Beispiele*.
7 Brown, *Performing*, p. 3, ref. 18.
8 Koury, *Orchestral Performance Practices*, p. 169.
9 The set of parts in the archives of the Tonkünstler-Societät, which Brown concludes was probably used for every large-scale performance conducted by the composer (Brown, *Performing*, p. 24), includes ten tenor and ten bass chorus parts (*ibid.*, p. 13), but none for the higher voices have survived. As one does not know whether any tenor or bass parts are also missing, this evidence in itself provides no secure basis for determining the likely proportions among the voices.
10 Brown, *Performing*, p. 13.
11 The additional part for a third flute in No. 29 would not have required an extra player since six flutists were already available.
12 Brown, *Performing*, Appendix 3.
13 *Ibid.*, Appendix 5.
14 Brown states (*Performing*, p. 28): 'The exact role of the continuo is left in an ambiguous state by the first edition, which demands only a keyboard realization in the dry recitatives.' In fact it does not distinguish between these and the rest of the music: in both, there is an unfigured bass marked 'Basso' or 'Bassi'. But the presence of a keyboard instrument is shown by the two 'senza cembalo' passages referred to above.
15 These are A:Wgm H 27405, called the 'Engraver's Score' by Brown, which has figures up to the middle of No. 6; and D-Ddr:B 9851, called the 'Estate Score' by Brown, which has full figures for most of Part One and for Nos. 16 and 34.
16 Koury, *Orchestral Performance Practices*, p. 104.
17 Clementi's realizations have been followed in my edition of the vocal score (London: Peters Edition, 1988).
18 Brown, *Performing*, pp. 28–9.
19 This is discussed in G. A. Macfarren's 1854 essay cited on p. 96 above.
20 Brown, *Performing*, p. 71.
21 'Nachrichten', *AMZ* 15 (1813), cols. 784–8.
22 Temperley, 'Haydn's Tempos'.
23 Brown, *Performing*, p. 44.
24 *Ibid.*, pp. 51, 61.
25 *Ibid.*, chap. 3.
26 There are seven such cases: No. 21, bars 6, 54; No. 29, bars 25, 27 and 59; No. 31, bars 26, 28.
27 Clearly it does not, for instance, when the last note under the slur is a semibreve or minim, is a dotted note, or is itself tied or slurred. In other circumstances there is uncertainty, unless the note carries a staccato dot, or is short and followed by a rest to make up the beat. For further discussion see Nicholas Temperley, 'Berlioz and the Slur', *Music & Letters* 50 (1969), pp. 388–92.
28 Brown, *Performing*, pp. 63–7.

Bibliography

Allgemeine musikalische Zeitung (AMZ) (Leipzig, 1798–1848)

Baumgärtner, Paula, 'Gottfried van Swieten als Textdichter von Haydns Oratorien' (dissertation, University of Vienna, 1930)

Blume, Friedrich, *Classic and Romantic Music: A Comprehensive Survey* (Kassel, 1958), trans. M. D. Herter (New York, 1970)

Brown, A. Peter, *Performing Haydn's* The Creation: *Reconstructing the Earliest Renditions* (Bloomington, Indiana, 1986)

Dean, Winton, *Handel's Dramatic Oratorios and Masques* (London, 1959)

Dies, Albert Christoph, *Biographische Nachrichten von Joseph Haydn* (Vienna, 1810); ed. H. Seeger (Berlin, [1959]); trans. in Gottwals, *Haydn*

Drury, Jonathan, 'Haydn's *Seven Last Words*: An Historical and Critical Study' (dissertation, University of Illinois, 1975)

Friedländer, Max, 'Van Swieten und das Textbuch zu Haydns "Jahreszeiten"', *Peters Jahrbuch 1909* (Leipzig, 1909), pp. 47ff

Geiringer, Karl (in collaboration with Irene Geiringer), *Haydn: A Creative Life in Music* (New York, 1946); 2nd edn rev. (Garden City, N.Y., 1963)

Geiringer, Karl, 'Haydn's Sketches for "The Creation"', *Musical Quarterly* 18 (1932), pp. 299–308

Gottwals, Vernon, ed., *Joseph Haydn: Eighteenth-Century Gentleman and Genius. A Translation . . . of the* Biographische Notizen über Joseph Haydn *by G. A. Griesinger and the* Biographische Nachrichten von Joseph Haydn *by A. C. Dies* (Madison, Wisconsin, 1963)

Griesinger, Georg August, *Biographische Notizen über Joseph Haydn* (Leipzig, 1810); ed. F. Grasberger (Vienna, 1954); trans. in Gottwals, *Haydn*

Hanslick, Eduard, *Geschichte des Concertwesens in Wien* (Vienna, 1869; repr. New York, 1979)

Hoboken, Anthony von, *Joseph Haydn: thematisch-bibliographisches Werkverzeichnis* (Mainz, 1957–78)

Koury, Daniel L., *Orchestral Performance Practices in the Nineteenth Century: Size, Proportions, and Seating* (Ann Arbor, 1986)

Landon, H. C. Robbins, *Haydn: Chronicle and Works*, vols II, *Haydn at Esterháza 1766–1790*; III, *Haydn in England 1791–1795*; IV, *Haydn: The*

Years of 'The Creation' 1796–1800; V, *Haydn: The Late Years 1801–1809* (London, 1976–80)

Le Huray, Peter, and James Day, *Music and Aesthetics in the Eighteenth and Early-Nineteenth Centuries* (Cambridge, 1981)

Levarie, Siegmund, 'The Closing Numbers of *Die Schöpfung*', in H. C. Robbins Landon, ed., *Studies in Eighteenth-Century Music: A Tribute to Karl Geiringer on his Seventieth Birthday* (New York, 1970), pp. 315–22

Milton, John, *Paradise Lost*, 2nd edn (London, 1674)

Mörner, C.-G. Stellan, 'Haydniana aus Schweden um 1800', *Haydn-Studien* 2 (1969), pp. 1–65

Myers, Rollo H., *Handel's Messiah: A Touchstone of Taste* (New York, 1948)

Nettl, Paul, *Mozart and Masonry* (New York, 1957)

Olleson, Edward, 'The Origin and Libretto of Haydn's *Creation*', *Haydn Yearbook 4* (1968), pp. 148–66

Pauly, Reinhard G., 'The Reforms of Church Music under Joseph II', *Musical Quarterly* 43 (1957), pp. 372–82

Pohl, Carl Ferdinand, *Mozart und Haydn in London* (Vienna, 1867; repr. New York, 1970)

Répertoire international des sources musicales (RISM), ser. A/I: *Einzeldrucke vor 1800*, ed. K. Schlager (Kassel, 1974)

Riedel-Martiny, Anke, 'Das Verhältnis von Text und Musik in Haydns Oratorien', *Haydn-Studien* 1 (1967), pp. 205–40

Rosen, Charles, *The Classical Style: Haydn, Mozart, Beethoven* (New York, 1972)

Rushton, Julian, *Classical Music: A Concise History from Gluck to Beethoven* (London, 1986)

Schenker, Heinrich, 'Haydn: Die Schöpfung. Die Vorstellung des Chaos', in Schenker, *Das Meisterwerk in der Musik*, vol. II (Munich, 1926), pp. 159–70

Schnorr, Hans, 'Das Oratorium von Ende des 18. Jahrhunderts bis 1880', in G. Adler, ed., *Handbuch der Musikgeschichte*, 2nd edn (Vienna, 1929; repr. Tutzing, 1961), pp. 927–39

Smith, Ruth M., 'Intellectual Contexts of Handel's Oratorios', in C. Hogwood and R. Luckett, eds. *Music in Eighteenth-Century England: Essays in Memory of Charles Cudworth* (Cambridge, 1983), pp. 115–33

Smither, Howard E., *A History of the Oratorio*, vol. III, *The Oratorio in the Classical Era* (Chapel Hill and London, 1987)

Steblin, Rita, *A History of Key Characteristics in the Eighteenth and Early Nineteenth Centuries* (Ann Arbor, 1983)

Stern, Martin, 'Haydns "Schöpfung": Geist und Herkunft des van Swieten-schen Librettos; ein Beitrag zum Thema "Säkularisation" im Zeitalter der Aufklärung', *Haydn-Studien* 1 (1965–7), pp. 121–98

Stromberg, Roland N., *Religious Liberalism in Eighteenth-Century England* (London, 1954)

Temperley, Nicholas, 'Haydn's Tempos in *The Creation*', forthcoming in *Early Music* (1991)

Temperley, Nicholas, 'New Light on the Libretto of *The Creation*', in C. Hogwood and R. Luckett, eds., *Music in Eighteenth-Century England: Essays in Memory of Charles Cudworth* (Cambridge, 1983), pp. 189–211

Tovey, Donald Francis, 'The Creation', in Tovey, *Esssays in Musical Analysis* (London, 1937), vol. V, pp. 114–46

Walter, Horst, 'Gottfried van Swietens handschriftliche Textbücher zu "Schöpfung" und "Jahreszeiten" ', *Haydn-Studien* 1 (1965–7), pp. 241–77

Weber, William, 'The 1784 Handel Commemoration as Political Ritual', *Journal of British Studies* 28 (1989), pp. 43–69

Index

Italic page references indicate main treatments.

A., P. L., 96
Addison, J., 10
Albrechtsberger, J. G., 2, 31–2
Anglicanism, 11–12
arias, *69–78*, 90–2, 97–98
  da capo aria, 24, 70–1
  transformed da capo, 70–1, 72–4
  rondò, 71, 78
  strophic aria, 71, 78
Artaria & Co., 38, 114
articulation, 116–17
Ashley, J., 21, 27, 39–40

Bach, J. S., 2, 47, 65, 108
Barthélemon, F. H., 31
Bartleman, J., 40
Beethoven, L. van, 44, 45, 105–6, 108
Berlioz, H., 43, 100
Bethlehem (Pennsylvania), 41
Biba, O., 111
Billroth, T., 44
Boccherini, G. G., 6
Boston (Massachusetts), 42
Breitkopf & Härtel, 8, 29, 38
Brown, A. P., 38, 109, *111–12*, 115, 116
Busby, T., 44, 94–5

choral festivals, English provincial, 4, 45, 109
choral forces, 36, 40, 110–11
choruses (movements), *78–82*, 92
Chubb, T., 11
Clementi, M., 38, 85, 113
continuo, 35, 36, *113–14*
THE CREATION/DIE SCHÖPFUNG
  composition, 32–5
  critical reception, 36, 40, *42–7*, 89–99, 103–8

editions, 36–9, 41, 45, 113, 114, *118*
first performance, 35
movement types, 65, 66, 70, 78, 82, 84
musical styles, *65–88*, 107–8
performance practice, 38–9, *109–17*
place in history, 1, 8, 46–7
sketches, *32–5*
text, *19–31*, 51–64
tonality, 49–51, 73, 77–8, 83, 86
Movements (identified, pp.119–20; full texts, pp. 52–64)
  No. 1: orchestral introduction, 35, 43, 50, *82–4*, *89–90*, 94, 99, *100–3*, *103–5*, *107–8*, 128(n.23); vocal portion, 22, 23, 30, 35, 36, 44, 50–1, 68, *79–80*, 93–4, 115–16
  No. 2, 13, 23, 26, 51, 70, 72, *74*, 79, 91, *97–8*, 110, 127 (nn.2, 3)
  No. 3, 22, 26, 67, 113, 118 (n.3)
  No. 4, 22, 23, 49, 70, 79, 110
  No. 5, 22, 65, 115
  No. 6, 32, 72, *73*, 114, 116
  No. 7, 22
  No. 8, 17, *72–3*, 105, 115
  No. 9, 22
  No. 10, 22, 80–1, 91
  No. 11, 22, 29
  No. 12, 11, 22, 23, 25, 67, 68, 91, 113
  No. 13, 11, 22, 25, 33, 40, 49, 80, *81–2*, 93, 105, 114
  No. 14, 22, 68, 115
  No. 15, 33, 72, *74*, 91, 124 (n.41)
  No. 16, 22, 33, *69–70*, 128 (n.15)
  No. 17, 22
  No. 18, 23, 72, *78*, 95, 113
  No. 19, 22, 80
  No. 20, 22
  No. 21, 67, *68*

No. 22, 13–14, 23, 72, *74–78*, 91, 95
No. 23, 22
No. 24, 51, 74, *74–7*, 97, 118
No. 25, 22
No. 26, 49, 66, 80, 81, 105
No. 27, 12, 23, 26, 33, 49, 91, 105, 113
No. 28, 20, 42, 51, 80–1, 91
No. 29, 49, 68, 82, 115, 128 (n.11)
No. 30, 14, 17, 23, 24, 27, 28, 33–4, 49, 78, 79, *84–8*, 105, 125 (n.76), 125–6, (n.1)
No. 31, 14, *65–6*, 115
No. 32, 14, 17, 23, 24, 29, 41, 44, *78*, 124 (n.41), 125 (n.76), 126 (n.14)
No. 33, 12, 27, 41, 105, 125 (n.67)
No. 34, 41, 80, 81, 110, 128 (n.15)
creationism, 9–10
Crotch, W., 43
Czerny, C., 41

Dean, W., 3–4
Deists, *11*, 12, 15
Delany, M., 20
Dies, A. C., 19
Dragonetti, D., 113
duet, 23–4, *78*
Dukas, P., 44, *100*
Dussek, S., 40
dynamics, 116

Edinburgh, 40, 46, 125 (n.67)
Elssler, J., 28, 35, 38
embellishment (vocal), 115
Enlightenment, 8, 14, *15*, 18, 50
Erard, 38
Esterházy, princes, 4, 5
Eybler, J. L., 2

freemasonry, *13*, 16
Friebert, J., 7
Friedländer, M., 28
fugues, 80–1, 92

Garat, P. J., 42
Gardiner, W., 44, 93–4
Geiringer, K., 45, 106–7
Gerardi, C., 35
Gesellschaft der Associierten, 2, 7, 32
Gesellschaft der Musikfreunde, 38, 42, 111
Goodwin, T., 39

Grabner, H., 125 (nn.74, 76)
Griesinger, G. A., 16, 19

Hamilton, N., 20
Handel, G. F., 1, 2, *3–4*, 14, 20, 42, 44, 94
    influence on Haydn, 5, 66–7, *78–81*, 107
    Acis and Galatea, 67
    Hercules, 79
    Israel in Egypt, 3–4, 5, 26, 65
    Joshua, 67
    Judas Macabaeus, 2
    Messiah, 3–4, 14, 26, 31, 47, 65, 67, 80
    Samson, 20, 49, 70, 81, 82
Handel Commemoration Festivals, 4, 36, 40
Hanslick, E., 44
Haydn, F. J., *4–5*, 16–18, 45–6
    masses, 7, 31, 83, 126 (n.14)
    oratorios, *5–8*
    piano trios, 31
    string quartets, 31, 45, 83
    symphonies, 42, 45, 83
    L'anima del filosofo, 126 (n.14)
    Armida, 67, 71, 126 (n.14)
    Orlando paladino, 71
    Il ritorno di Tobia, 2, *5–6*, 49, 67, 78, 94, 126 (n.6)
    The Seasons/Die Jahreszeiten, 2, *8*, 30, 46, 49, 96
    The Seven Last Words, 2, *6–7*, 31, 49, 96
    see also THE CREATION
Herschel, W., 104–5
Hook, T., 82
Hume, D., 11
Hymn (movement in *The Creation*), *84–8*
hymn tunes, 11, 82, 86

Incledon, C., 40

Joseph II, Emperor, 15–16

Kant, E., 104

Landon, H. C. R., 32–5, 45, 50
Langley, L., 95
language of text, 19, 109–10
Laplace, P. S., 104
Larsen, J. P., 45
Leibniz, G. W., 15
Leopold II, emperor, 36
Lessing, G. E., 15
Levarie, S., 17–18, 49, 78

libretto
  authorship, 19–20
  character, 12–13
  style, 24–6, 89
Lindley, R., 113–14
Linley, T. (the elder), 20
Locke, J., 10
London, *3–4*, 39–40
  Handel Commemorations, 4, 36, 40
  oratorio concerts, 4, 40, 111
  Sacred Harmonic Society, 45

Macfarren, G. A., 45, *96–98*
Mara, G., 40
Metastasio, P., 2, 25
Milton, J., *13–14*, 20, 22, 25, 40
Mozart, W. A., 2, 23, 84
  orchestration of Handel's oratorios, 2
  Così fan tutte, 48, 71
  Il Davidde penitente, 2
  Die Entführung aus dem Serail, 2
  Fantasia in C minor (K. 475), *84–5*
  Idomeneo, 71
  The Magic Flute, 6, 16, 67
  Piano Concerto in C minor, 85

Napoleon I, emperor, 40
Neukomm, S., 38, 113, 114
New York, 42
Newton, I., 10
nonconformists, 12, 45
Norwich, 40

Olleson, E., 19, 20
opera buffa, 71, 118 (n.14)
opera seria, 6, 9, 23, 66, *70–1*, 72
oratorio, 1, 26
  German, 2, 7, 16
  English, *3–4*
  Italian, 1, 66
  Viennese, *1–3*
Oratorio Concerts (London), 4, 39–40, 111
orchestral forces, 37, 41, 113–14
orchestral movements in *The Creation*, *82–3*
ornaments, 115

Page, J., 40
Paris, *40–1*, 43, 111
pastoral convention, 46, 68, 82, *108*
Peter, J. F., 42
piano, 113

Pleyel, I., 38, 40

Rathmayer, M., 35
recitative
  accompanied, 6, 7, *66–70*
  secco, *65–6*, 113, 115–16
La recréation du monde, 41
religious music, 3, 9, 97
Rey, J. B., 41
Roman Catholic Church, 15
Romanticism, 43–4, 84
rondò, 71, 74, 78
Rosen, C., 46, 82, *107–8*

Saal, I., 35
Saal, T., 36
Sacred Harmonic Society, 45
Salieri, A., 35, 114
Salomon, J. P., 21, 25, 27, 31, 35, 39–40
Schelling, F. W. J. von, 43
Schenker, H., 44, *100–3*
Schiller, J. C. F. von, 27, 125 (n.80)
Schlegel, J. A., 15
Schopenhauer, A., 43
Schubart, C. F. D., 51
Schwarzenberg, Prince J. zu, 35
Second, M., 40
Ségur, J., 41
Silverstolpe, F. S., 24, 32, 35
singspiel, 2, 71, 126 (n.14)
Smart, Sir G., 40, 113
Smith, J. C., 20
Smith, R., 4
Smither, H., 5–6, 49, 67, 71, 122 (n.17)
soloists (vocal), 35–6, 40, 41, *110*
Spohr, L., 40
Stael, A. L. G. N. de, 43
Steibelt, D., 41
Stern, M., *15*, 28
Stillingfleet, B., 20
Sullivan, A., 106
Swieten, Baron G. van, *2*, 9, 16, 31, 104
  concerts, 2
  libretto for *The Seasons*, 8
  part in *The Creation*, 19, 21–4, *26–30*, 32,
    38, 66, 67, 70
  translations, 2, 8, 30

Taylor, E., *95–6*
tempo, 114
terzetto, 78

Thomson, J., 8
Thonmalerei, see tone-painting
tone-painting, 6, 42, 43, 44, 67–8, *72–4*,
   100, 108
Tonkünstler-Societät, 2, 5, 36, 44, 111–12
Tovey, D., 45–7, 82, 84, *103–7*, 125 (nn.67,
   76)
trio, 78

Uz, J. P., 15

Vienna,. *1–3*, 16, 35–8, 44, 96
   Gesellschaft der Associierten, 2, 7,
      32
   Gesellschaft der Musikfreunde, 38, 42,
      111

Tonkünstler-Societät, 2, 5, 36, 44,
   111–12
university, 36, 109

Wagner, R., 83
Weigl, J., 36
Wesley, J., 12
Whiston, W., 10
Wolf, H., 44, *98–9*
Wölfl, J., 39
word-painting, *see* tone-painting
Wranitzky, A., 38

York, 40

Zelter, C. F., 42, *89–92*